West Acader
Emeritus A

Agency and Partnership

David Simon Sokolow
The University of Texas School of Law

A SHORT & HAPPY GUIDE® SERIES

WEST
ACADEMIC
PUBLISHING

a short & happy guide series is a trademark registered in the U.S. Patent and Trademark Office.

© 2021 LEG, Inc. d/b/a West Academic
    444 Cedar Street, Suite 700
    St. Paul, MN 55101
    1-877-888-1330
Printed in the United States of America

ISBN: 978-1-62810-148-5

To my wife, Tobi, my partner in every sense of the word

Acknowledgments

First and foremost, I would like to thank the thousands of students in my Business Associations class at The University of Texas School of Law over the last 40 years, especially those with little or no business background. Their "I have no clue what you are talking about" quandary forced me to find creative ways to explain complicated business statutes and the impact of those statutes out in the real world. You made me a better teacher.

I would particularly like to thank Bonnie Devany, UT '22, and Benjamin Ediger, UT '22, for their editorial assistance and substantive suggestions for improvement. They were instrumental in making the book more accessible to its target audience.

I would also like to thank my "team" at West: Louis Higgins, who signed me up to write the book (alas, no signing bonus) and Megan Putler, Megan Hoffman, and Greg Olson, the editors and production manager who brought the book to life.

Finally, I would like to acknowledge my assistant, Nancy Bennett, who consistently keeps me honest; my wife, Tobi, whose astute observations improved the book enormously; and my son, Adam, for his loving support and wicked sense of humor.

About the Author

David Simon Sokolow has taught Business Associations and Contracts at The University of Texas School of Law for forty years. A five-time winner of the Teacher-of-the-Year award, he has lectured for BARBRI for more than three decades on A&P, Contracts, and Corporations. From 2003-2013, he was U.T.'s Director of Student Life, creating and implementing programs to foster community and reduce stress at the law school. He earned his B.A., M.A. (art history), and J.D. at Columbia. Before coming to U.T., he clerked for The Honorable Thomas Gibbs Gee of the Fifth Circuit and practiced Entertainment Law at Paul, Weiss, Rifkind, Wharton & Garrison in New York. After teaching B.A. for a while, he realized he could benefit from having more business background, so he went to school on weekends to earn an M.B.A. at U.T. He has been a visiting professor at Emory, Ohio State, S.M.U. and Case Western Reserve, and taught Art Law abroad for the University of San Diego and St. Mary's. He loves his wife, his son and teaching, not necessarily in that order!

Introduction

I usually have more than 100 students in my B.A. class. They fall into two categories: (1) students with business background who intend to practice transactional law; and (2) students with no business background whatsoever who are taking B.A. because it's a "bar course." Imagine how hard it is to teach a course with such a bifurcated audience. How do you bring inexperienced students up to speed without losing the others? Believe me, it is an unenviable task.

Early on in my teaching career, I decided to gear my class to students who lack business experience. By the end of the semester, I want them to understand how a business transaction works, even if they do not intend to practice transactional law.

Business law sounds exciting, but the daily grind of parsing partnership and corporate statutes can frankly be a drag (as I am sure you already know!). It is up to me to generate interest by giving real-life examples, mapping out complicated relationships and providing a framework for applying complex statutory material. That is essentially what I do here. I also address policy. In my view, understanding the policy underlying a statute makes it easier to grasp why the statute reads as it does and whether the statute succeeds in achieving its goal.

Corporations are all over the news. Partnerships, not so much. Yet, those of you who do not plan to represent large, public corporations are far more likely to encounter a variety of partnerships in your law practice or day-to-day life. This book will be invaluable in that regard. You will learn to differentiate a general partnership from a limited liability partnership from a limited partnership. The practical consequences of choosing to operate a business in one form rather than another may surprise you, but you will have mastered the distinctions by the time you finish this book.

Agency used to be a required first-year class, but it is now shoehorned into the course on Business Associations. There was a reason agency was a required course: agency principles are vitally important in the real world, not only for businesses, but for individuals as well. People appoint agents to act on their behalf. Often, an agent enters a contract on behalf of someone else (who is known as a "principal"). Occasionally, an agent may commit a tort. Analyzing agency in a contract context requires a different methodology from analyzing agency in a tort setting. I lay it all out here in a straightforward manner that is easy to apply on your final exam or on the bar. Sit back and enjoy the ride!

Table of Contents

PART II. GENERAL PARTNERSHIP LAW

PART III. LIMITED PARTNERSHIPS

PART IV. CHOICE OF BUSINESS FORM: LLP OR LLC?

PART V. A FINAL NOTE

A Short & Happy Guide to
Agency and Partnership

PART I

Agency Law

CHAPTER 1

Agency Law Overview

An agency relationship involves the delegation of responsibility or authority by one person, the "principal," to another person, the "agent." In practical terms, the agent acts in a representative capacity, on behalf of the principal.

Business associations can only act through agents. A partnership, for example, cannot enter a contract unless a partner (or someone else authorized to act for the partnership) executes a contract on its behalf. The same is true for a corporation or a limited liability company. Accordingly, agency law applies to a business association, as principal, the people acting for the business association, as its agents, and the third parties with whom the agents interact.

However, agency law applies to individuals as well as business associations. An actor or athlete may hire an agent to get him a job. You may hire a real estate agent to help you buy or sell a house. As a result, the agency principles explored below apply to *any* agency relationship, not only to agency relationships involving a business association.

We will first look at what *is* required to establish an agency relationship and then acknowledge what *is not* essential to establishing the relationship. Our overview will conclude with an introduction to the all-important distinction between agency law in a tort setting versus agency law in a contract context.

A. What Is Required: Consent and Control

There are two pre-requisites for an agency relationship to exist: (1) consent and (2) control. First, to establish and maintain an agency relationship, both the principal and the agent must *consent* to the agent's acting on the principal's behalf. The consent of the principal alone or the agent alone is not sufficient. Consent may be oral, written or implied from a party's conduct.

Once the principal and agent consent, their agency relationship will continue until either one withdraws his consent (unless the power of agency is irrevocable, as discussed in "Termination of Authority" below).

Second, an agency relationship requires the agent to be subject to the principal's *control*. Many courts have construed this requirement to mean that the principal must have the *right* to control the way the agent performs the task, not that the principal must actually *exercise* control over the agent's performance.

B. What Is *Not* Required: Consideration and a Writing

While consent and control are required to establish an agency relationship, agency law does *not* require that an agent receive consideration (payment) for his services or that any agreement between the principal and agent be memorialized in a writing.

In the real world, most agents are paid for their services. Real estate agents usually get a commission of six percent of the sales price. Talent/sports agents generally get fifteen percent of the client's income from work secured by the agent. However, the principal does not have to give the agent consideration (compensation) to establish an agency relationship as a matter of law. Put another way, an agent may serve *gratuitously*. This explains why it is said that an agency relationship requires an *agreement* (mutual consent), but not a *contract* (no consideration).

Similarly, under agency law, no writing is necessary to form an agency relationship. However, contract law's Statute of Frauds may require a writing.

Under the Statute of Frauds, certain contracts may be enforced only if they are evidenced by a satisfactory writing. To satisfy the Statute of Frauds, a writing must (1) be signed by the party against whom enforcement of the contract is sought (the defendant) and (2) contain all the material terms of the contract. A plaintiff needs a writing signed by the *defendant* to persuade the court that the plaintiff is not making the whole thing up. Inclusion of all the material terms provides additional support for that premise.

One example of a type of contract that falls within the Statute of Frauds (*i.e.*, that requires a writing) is a contract that cannot be fully performed within one year from the date the contract is made (aka the "one-year prong" of the Statute of Frauds). So, if the principal and agent agree that their relationship will last for two years, the partnership agreement must be evidenced by a writing to satisfy the Statute of Frauds even though no writing is required under the law of agency.

C. Tort Versus Contract

Agency issues may arise in tort or in contract. These alternatives will be discussed in depth below, but for now, a summary will suffice.

1. *Tort Liability*

An agent injures a third party. As the tortfeasor, the agent is liable to the third party for any resulting injury or damage. The issue under agency law is whether the principal will be liable to the third party for the agent's tort, too. A typical case involves a tort committed by an employee. Thus, the question is usually whether the employer will *also* be liable to the injured third party for the employee's tort. As we shall see, the answer depends on whether the tort was committed by a *servant* within the *scope of the servant's employment*.

2. *Contract Liability*

Things work differently in a contract case. When an agent enters a contract with a third party, the primary issue is whether the principal is liable to the third party on that contract. The answer here depends on whether the agent had authority to contract for the principal (either *actual authority* or *apparent authority*) at the time of the contract or, if not, whether the principal *ratified* or *adopted* the contract after the fact. Actual authority, apparent authority, ratification, and adoption are the four ways in which a principal can become liable to a third party.

The principal's liability to the third party is not the only issue in a contract case. Other issues that may arise in a contract setting include the *third party's liability* to the principal on the contract, the *agent's liability* to the third party on the contract, and the *duties* the principal and agent owe one another. All these issues are addressed in depth below.

CHAPTER 2

Tort Liability

People in business cannot do everything themselves. Often, they must hire help. The relationship between employers and employees is regulated in part by labor law, but that subject is beyond the scope of this book. The question arising under agency law is whether an employer will be held liable to an injured party for a tort committed by one of his employees. This kind of second-hand liability is often referred to as "vicarious liability." Under vicarious liability, a person may be held liable for the wrongful act of another person with whom he has a *special relationship*. In our case, the special relationship is the employment relationship between employer and employee. Vicarious liability is sometimes referred to as "imputed negligence." Through this lens, the issue is whether the employee's negligence will be *imputed* to the employer. Different names, same game.

You may be wondering: why in the world would the employer be liable for the employee's tort? Isn't the employee liable to the injured party? Of course, the employee is liable! After all, the employee is the one who committed the tort. However, agency law imposes liability on the employer as well in certain circumstances. In those instances, the employer's "deep pocket" provides an additional source of recovery for the victim. This type of vicarious liability is sometimes referred to as *"respondeat superior"* (Latin for "let the master answer"). This term signifies that the party in a superior position (in our case, the employer) is held liable for the wrongful act of a subordinate (in our case, the employee) because of the special relationship between them.

There are two policy reasons to hold an employer liable for the torts of an employee. The first is that the employer is better able to absorb the costs of damages and can distribute those costs to the public in the form of higher prices or protect against them by purchasing liability insurance. The second reason is that an employer who is held strictly liable for the torts of an employee may have a greater incentive to exercise care in the hiring and supervision of his employees.

The critical question is: *when* is an employer liable for an employee's tort? Here is a diagram of a typical tort case:

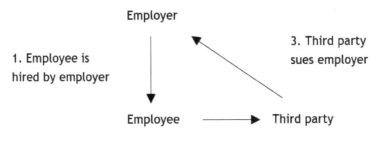

1. The employer hires the employee.

2. In the course of his employment (discussed in the next section) the employee commits a tort, negligently injuring a third party.

3. The injured party sues the employer on the tort.

Agency in a tort context involves a special vocabulary that has an archaic ring to it: the terms "master" and "servant" are used to refer to the principal and the agent respectively. It is always a good idea to use tort terminology in a fact pattern involving a tort to let your professor and the bar examiners know from the get-go that you are on their wavelength.

A. The Issues

The general rule is that a master is liable to an injured third party on a tort committed by a "servant" if the servant was acting within the scope of employment when the tort occurred. Thus, the appropriate framework for analyzing an agency problem in tort is encapsulated in the following two questions:

1. Was the tort committed by a **servant or an independent contractor**?

2. If the tort was committed by a servant, was the servant acting **within the scope of its employment** when the tort occurred?

We will examine each of these issues below.

B. Servant or Independent Contractor?

Distinguishing between a **servant** and an **independent contractor** is not an easy feat. Unfortunately, there is no bright-line test for when a tortfeasor will be considered a servant and when he will be considered an independent contractor. Resolution of the issue depends on the particular facts of a case. Still, some general observations are instructive.

An independent contractor generally has a task to complete, but it is up to the contractor to determine how to accomplish that task. In that sense, an independent contractor is relatively free of the employer's control. Thus, although the employer may dictate the *end result*, the employer does not dictate the *means* to achieve that end goal. As a result, an employer is not liable for a tort committed by an independent contractor, with a few rare exceptions. For example, if an employer *authorizes* an independent contractor to commit a tort the employer will be vicariously liable for the tort. Similarly, if an employer delegates to an independent contractor a *non-delegable duty* (often involving hazardous activity) the employer will be vicariously liable for the independent contractor's tort, too.

A servant, by contrast, is subject to the principal's control. The principal can dictate both the end goal *and* the means to get there. In that sense, a servant is *not* independent of the master.

1. *Factors to Consider*

In resolving the servant-or-independent contractor issue, courts look at a variety of factors that vary from one jurisdiction to another, making it difficult to summarize the relevant caselaw. Still, the Second Restatement of Agency § 220(2) provides a useful list of factors to consider in determining whether an employee is a servant or an independent contractor, some of which we will examine in-depth. The Restatement, however, is not a statute, so courts are not obligated to apply it. Regardless, the Restatement is a highly persuasive authority that is frequently cited by the courts, so it serves as a useful guide in this area. Accordingly, it makes sense to explore the most significant Restatement factors.

Employer's right to control: The employer's control over, or his right to control, the details of the employee's work, is by far the most significant factor in this inquiry. Section 220(1) of the Second Restatement of Agency defines a "servant" as "a person employed to perform services in the affairs of another and who with respect to the physical conduct in the performance of the services is subject to the other's control or *right to control*" (emphasis added).

Relevant caselaw confirms that the employer need not actually exercise control over the employee's performance for the employee to be considered a servant. The mere *right* of the employer to control the details of an employee's activities is usually sufficient to establish a master-servant relationship.

Example #1

The owner of a grocery store hires a clerk to perform routine tasks, like stocking shelves and cleaning up. The owner could spell out when and how to perform each task, but instead lets the clerk make these decisions himself. The clerk is a servant because the owner has the *right* to control the details of how the clerk performs the job, even if the owner has not actually exercised control over the clerk.

Even if a contract expressly provides that an employee is an independent contractor, a court may nevertheless conclude that the employee is a servant if the employer has the right to control the way the employee does the job. Courts are not constrained by what may be a self-serving characterization in the employment contract designed to absolve the employer of vicarious liability for the employee's torts. The facts, not the declaration in the contract, are determinative.

Skill: The less skill required to do a particular job, the more likely the employee is to be deemed a servant. Unskilled laborers will almost certainly be considered servants.

Regularity of payment: If an employee is paid on a regular basis, like a wage or a salary, the employee is more likely to be characterized as a servant. Conversely, if the employee is paid by the job in a lump sum, the employee is more likely to be viewed as an independent contractor.

Employer's regular business: If the job was part of the employer's regular business operations, the employee is more likely to be considered a servant. An independent contractor is usually hired to handle a special assignment or an unusual task.

Separate trade or business: If the employee is engaged in a separate trade or business, the employee is more likely to be classified as an independent contractor. A "Jack-of-all-trades" employee who lacks a distinct trade or business will most likely be viewed as a servant.

Duration: If the employment is relatively long-term, the employee is more likely to be considered a servant. In that case, it looks like the employment involves a regular full-time job.

Kind of occupation: If the work is usually done under the direction of the employer, the employee is more likely to be a servant. Conversely, if the work is usually done by a specialist without supervision, the employee is more likely an independent contractor.

Tools and workplace: If the employer supplies the employee with tools and a place to work, the employee is more likely to be a servant. Independent contractors usually have their own tools and often work on their own premises.

Keep in mind that this list is not an exclusive enumeration of all the factors that courts consider in assessing scope of employment. The list merely identifies the *primary* factors cited by courts with respect to this issue and included in the Second Restatement's compilation.

2. *Third Restatement of Agency*

In a surprising about-face, the Third Restatement of Agency abandoned the terms "master" and servant." The Third Restatement substitutes the term "employee agent" for "servant," and "non-employee agent" for "independent contractor." Despite the new vocabulary, the substantive analysis for distinguishing an employee agent from a non-employee agent is pretty much the same.

Regardless of this change in terminology, use of the terms "master," "servant," and "independent contractor" is so deeply ingrained in agency jurisprudence that courts are likely to continue to rely on those terms for the foreseeable future. More importantly, so will your professors!

C. Scope of Employment

Once a plaintiff has established that an employer had the right to control an employee, the plaintiff must then show that at the time of the tortious conduct, the employee was acting *within the scope of his employment.*

Even though a tort was committed by a servant, the master is not automatically liable to a third party for the servant's tort. That kind of blanket liability would not be fair to the master. After all, the master is not omniscient; unlike Santa, he cannot see when the servant is sleeping and when the servant is awake. For example, if an employee has a fender-bender while he is away on vacation, the employer will not be liable for the employee's negligence.

A master will be vicariously liable for the servant's tort only if the servant committed the tort *within the scope of the servant's employment.* In other words, the master's liability for a servant's torts is limited to torts that are somehow related to the task or tasks the master hired the servant to do. This, of course, makes sense because one of the underlying policies of *respondeat superior* is to provide an incentive for the master to exercise care in the selection, training, and supervision of its servants.

1. *Authorized Conduct*

For an employee's conduct to be considered within the scope of employment, the conduct must be of the same general nature as, or incidental to, the conduct authorized by the employer. Under Section 228 of the Second Restatement of Agency, conduct is authorized so long as the conduct is:

— of the kind the servant was authorized to perform;

— occurs substantially within the authorized time and space limits; and

— is performed, at least in part, by a purpose to serve the master.

Thus, if the servant was performing its usual tasks for the purpose of serving the master when the tort occurred, a court will consider the tort to have been committed within the scope of employment.

Example #2

While restocking shelves in the grocery store, the clerk accidentally drops a carton of milk on the floor. A nearby customer slips on the spilled milk and breaks her leg. The shop owner will be liable for the clerk's negligence because the clerk was simply doing his job when the accident occurred.

2. *Similar or Incidental Conduct*

Factors to be considered in determining if conduct is similar or incidental to the conduct authorized by the principal are listed in the Second Restatement of Agency § 229(2):

— whether or not the act is one commonly done by servants;

— the time, place and purpose of the act;

— the previous relations between the master and the servant;

— the extent to which the business of the master is apportioned between different servants;

— whether or not the act is outside the enterprise of the master or, if within the enterprise, has not been entrusted to any servant;

— the similarity in quality of the act done to the act authorized;

— whether or not the instrumentality by which the harm is done has been furnished by the master to the servant;

— the extent of departure from the normal method of accomplishing an authorized result; and

— whether or not the act is seriously criminal.

There is no bright line test for determining whether a servant was acting within the scope of employment. Resolution of this issue depends on the facts of a particular case. Comment a to Section 229 of the Second Restatement of Agency identifies the "ultimate question" regarding the scope of employment: "whether or not it is just that the loss resulting from the servant's acts should be considered as one the normal risks to be borne by the business in which the servant is employed." This provides a useful standard for framing the "scope of employment" issue.

3. *Detour and Frolic*

Shifting gears, the Second Restatement of Agency § 228(2) notes that conduct is *not* within the scope of employment if it is "different in kind from that authorized, far beyond the authorized time and space limits, or too little actuated by a purpose to serve the master."

Where a servant has deviated from his ordinary tasks when he commits a tort, a court will assess *how substantial* the servant's deviation was. If the deviation was minor (known as a **"detour"**), a court will usually ignore that the servant had strayed from its ordinary tasks and conclude that the tort was *within* the scope of employment.

Example #3

The clerk takes a five-minute smoking break outside the store's entrance, and accidentally burns a customer entering the premises. The court will likely disregard the fact that the clerk was on a break and hold the employer liable to the customer for the clerk's negligence, given the temporal and physical proximity of the accident to the clerk's employment.

On the other hand, if the deviation was substantial (colorfully known as a **"frolic"**), a court will likely find that the tort was committed *outside* the scope of employment, so the employer will *not* be vicariously liable for the tort. In essence, the court absolves the master from vicarious liability because the servant strayed so far from his ordinary tasks. The link between the employer and the tort is simply too attenuated to impose liability on the master.

Example #4

Amazon Prime hires Joey to makes deliveries. In the middle of his shift, Joey drives to a pub seven miles off his route to meet friends for a beer. *As he approaches the pub*, Joey runs a stop sign and injures a pedestrian. A court will likely conclude that Amazon Prime is not liable for Joey's negligence because was on a *frolic* when the accident occurred. Joey's deviation was substantial (seven miles away from his route) and was for his personal purposes, not in furtherance of Amazon Prime's business.

Be aware that an employee who goes on a frolic may *re-enter* the scope of his employment when he is reasonably near the authorized space and time limits and is acting with the purpose of serving the master's business. In other words, the frolic may have ended by the time the employee commits the tort.

Example #5

The same facts as Example #4, except that the accident does not occur until after Joey leaves the pub and is *returning to his route*. Joey completes his route by his usual stopping time. On these facts, a court may conclude that Amazon Prime *is* liable for Joey's negligence on the theory that Joey had *reentered* the scope of his employment by the time the accident occurred. Not only was Joey on the way back to his route, but the accident did not interfere with finishing his deliveries on time. As between the employer and the pedestrian, the court may tip the scales in favor of the injured party.

---

4. Coming-and-Going Rule

Under what is commonly known as the *"coming-and-going rule,"* a servant is *not* acting within the scope of employment while commuting to and from work. Anything that transpires during the commute is considered to have happened on the employee's own time.

5. Borrowed Servant Doctrine

A related issue to scope of employment arises when a master loans a servant to another person, and the servant commits a tort. Who is liable to the injured party, the original master or the borrower master?

The answer is provided by the **borrowed servant doctrine**. This doctrine imposes liability on the *borrower* master if he had the *right to control* the servant at the time the servant committed the tort. As mentioned above, the right to control an employee's conduct is the most significant factor in distinguishing a servant from an independent contractor. The right to control is equally important in the borrowed servant context. The issue is whether the *original* master or the *borrower* master had the right to control the servant when the servant committed the tort. Thus, the original master's vicarious liability risk ceases when the borrower master obtains the right to control the servant.

Example #6

Padma borrows Tom's full-time chef to cook for a charity event she is hosting. During the festivities, the chef negligently injures a guest with a carving knife. Assuming the chef was working in Padma's kitchen under her supervision, it is reasonable to assume Padma had the right to control the chef when the accident occurred. As a result, Padma would be vicariously liable to the injured guest for the chef's negligence. The chef would be liable for his own negligence, too. Tom would be off the hook.

6. Servant's Intentional Torts

Holding the master liable for the servant's negligence is one thing, but the servant's intentional torts are another matter entirely. The servant's intentional torts are almost always considered to have been committed *outside* the scope of employment. In agency lingo, the servant's intent is not "imputed" to the master. The only person responsible for the servant's intentional tort is the servant himself.

Well, almost. . . . The master *will* be vicariously liable for a servant's intentional tort in two limited circumstances: (1) where the master encouraged or authorized the servant to commit an intentional tort or (2) where the master could reasonably expect the employee to commit a tort given the nature of the employee's job. *See* Second Restatement of Agency § 228(1)(d).

Example #7

A bouncer at a bar injures a patron while in the process of expelling the patron from the premises. The owner could reasonably expect the bouncer to commit a tort given the nature of what a bouncer does: throwing unruly customers out of the bar. As a result, the bar owner will be vicariously liable to the expelled patron for the bouncer's intentional tort.

D. Liability: Joint and Several

If a servant committed a tort within the scope of employment, the master and the servant will be **jointly and severally liable** to the injured third party. "Joint and several" liability means that the third-party plaintiff has a choice: he can choose to *join* the master and servant as defendants and sue them both at the same time (joint liability) or he can opt to sue *either* the master alone *or* the servant alone for the full amount of his damages (several liability). Thus, in Example #6 above (the borrowed servant hypo), the injured guest could join the chef and Padma as defendants in the lawsuit and sue them both at the same time (joint liability) or the guest could sue either the chef alone, or Padma alone, for the full amount of his damages (several liability). Agency law has a lot of sympathy for tort claimants.

Keep in mind, however, that a third party is entitled to only *one total recovery*. He cannot recover the full amount of his damages from the master, then turn around and recover the full amount from the servant (or vice versa). Agency law is not *that* sympathetic to tort claimants—no "double-dipping" allowed!

It is *several* liability that provides the injured party with access to the master's "deep pocket." Yes, the master is entitled to be reimbursed by the servant for any damages the master must pay the injured party. That makes perfect sense—the servant committed the tort and therefore should have to ultimately bear the burden of his negligence. But if the servant does not have any resources, the master is left "holding the bag."

In Example #6, if the injured guest sues Padma severally, Padma can recover whatever she has to pay the guest from the chef who committed the tort. Unfortunately, if the chef has no assets with which to repay Padma, Padma must bear the brunt of the guest's damages. As between the wealthy master and the injured third party, the law tips the scales in favor of the injured third party. The injured third party can go against the master, and the master in turn can go against the servant, but if the servant is insolvent, the master takes the hit, not the "innocent" third party.

E. Master's *Direct* Liability

We have been exploring an employer's *vicarious* liability for an employee's tort. However, an employer may be *directly* liable for its own negligence.

Direct liability is a separate issue from vicarious liability. Direct liability attaches when an employer could have prevented the tort but failed to act. The most common example of direct liability is where an employer fails to check the tortfeasor's criminal record or job history in advance to see if any problems had surfaced in the past. Had the employer checked, he probably would not have hired the tortfeasor and the tort would have never occurred.

Here is a typical illustration. Pizza Hut hires Dominic Toretto (from the "Fast and Furious" franchise) as a driver, without checking his driving record. Unfortunately, Dominic had accumulated multiple citations for reckless driving. Dominic has a fender-bender while on a frolic. Pizza Hut will not be *vicariously* liable to anyone injured by Dominic's negligence because Dominic was acting outside the scope of his employment on his frolic. However, Pizza Hut will still be *directly* liable for its own negligence in hiring Domenic. A reasonable employer would have checked out Dominic's driving record before hiring him to work as a delivery person. Because Pizza Hut failed to do that, Pizza Hut will be liable for the damage caused by *its own* negligence, not for any negligence on Dominic's part.

Direct liability may also arise in other circumstances where an employer should have known better than to do what the employer did (or did not do). For example, direct liability will arise if an employer fails to properly train or supervise its employees or hires an employee who is not qualified to do the job. Likewise, direct liability will result if the employer gives ambiguous or contradictory instructions to an employee. In each case, imposing direct liability on the employer is appropriate because the accident or injury would likely never have occurred if the employer had properly supervised its employees, hired a qualified employee, or dispensed clear instructions to the employee. Although we can never know for certain what would have happened in these circumstances, the employer is held responsible regardless.

CHAPTER 3

Contract Liability

In a contract setting, the primary issue is whether a principal is liable to a third party on a contract executed by an agent on the principal's behalf. This complicated issue can be summarized in a single sentence: A principal will be liable to a third party on a contract entered into by an agent if the agent had *actual or apparent authority* to bind the principal when the agent executed the contract or if the principal *ratified or adopted* the contract later on.

On your Business Associations final or the bar exam, let your professor or the bar examiners know immediately that you are on their wavelength by posing the following questions:

1. Did the agent have **actual authority** to act for the principal when the agent executed the contract?

2. Did the agent have **apparent authority** to act for the principal when the agent executed the contract?

3. Did the principal **ratify** the contract after the fact?

4. Did the principal **adopt** the contract after the fact?

If you answer any of these questions in the affirmative, the principal is bound to the third party on the contract. Taking this straight-forward approach at the outset lets the reader know you have an analytical framework with which to approach the problem. You are well on your way to an "A." Still, exploring the concepts of actual authority, apparent authority, ratification, and adoption at greater length is instructive. In this arena, less is *not* more; more is more!

A. Actual Authority

1. Terminology

Although it is only two words long, the term **"actual authority"** is redundant. Actual authority is synonymous with "authority," as defined in the Second Restatement of Agency § 7. If a principal has in fact authorized an agent to act on the principal's behalf, the agent has *authority* to act for the principal.

For practical reasons, however, we use the term "actual authority" to distinguish "authority" from **"apparent authority."** Apparent authority arises where a principal creates the *appearance* that an agent has authority to bind him when in fact the agent has no authority to bind the principal at all. In this book, the term "actual authority" is used to maintain that distinction.

Actual authority involves three requirements: (1) The authority must be conferred by the principal on the agent (either expressly or impliedly) (2) to conduct the specified action on behalf of the principal, (3) which the principal would otherwise have had the capacity to do on his own. Actual authority may be express or implied. What's the difference?

2. *Express Actual Authority*

Actual authority is conferred by the principal on the agent. Actual authority may be express or implied. **Express actual authority** is created by the principal's *words* to the agent, as where the principal *tells* the agent to act on his behalf.

Example #1
I tell my research assistant to charge books at the university bookstore to my in-house account. I have given my RA *express actual authority* to charge books at the university bookstore to my in-house account.

3. *Implied Actual Authority*

Implied actual authority arises when the *agent* draws a reasonable inference from principal's *conduct* that the agent has authority to act on the principal's behalf, even though the principal has never *told* the agent to act for him in that way. This involves a *reasonable person* standard—if the principal's conduct would lead a reasonable person in the agent's position to believe the agent had authority to act on the principal's behalf, then the agent had implied actual authority to do so.

Example #2
A few days after my research assistant charged the books to my account in Example #1, I ask him to get some additional books. This time, however, I do not tell my RA he can charge the books to my account. Because my RA has previously charged books to my account, it is reasonable for him to believe that he has the authority to do it again. My RA thus has *implied actual authority* to charge my bookstore account based on the previous transaction.

Here is a diagram of how actual authority operates:

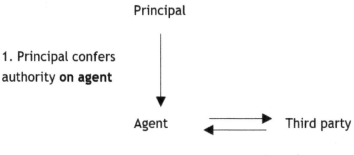

1. The principal confers authority on the agent (expressly or impliedly).

2. The agent contracts with a third party on the principal's behalf.

Result: The principal is bound to the third party on the contract.

4. *Specific Action*

For the principal to be bound on the contract, the agent must have had actual authority to take the *specific action* the agent ended up taking. It is not enough that the principal gave the agent actual authority to do *something*.

Example #3

Tyra authorizes Vanna to sell a piece of property for a *minimum price* of $300,000. Tyra tells interested buyers to contact Vanna. Vanna contracts to sell the property for $275,000 to one of those interested buyers. When Tyra learns the price, she refuses to convey the property to the buyer, claiming Vanna lacked actual authority to sell it for $275,000. Tyra is correct. Actual authority exists only if Vanna was authorized to take the *specific action* she took. It is not enough that Vanna was authorized to sell Tyra's property. The crucial question is whether Vanna was authorized to sell it *for $275,000*. Because the answer is no, the buyer cannot hold Tyra to the $275,000 contract based on Vanna's actual authority. However, the buyer has another arrow in his quiver: apparent authority (see below).

5. Incidental Authority

Incidental authority gives the agent the right to do whatever is necessary to accomplish the underlying task. Put another way, incidental authority *comes along with* actual authority.

Example #4
A landlord hires someone to manage an office building knowing the task is more than one person can handle. The landlord's grant of authority to manage the building therefore carries with it the right to hire a janitorial staff, purchase security equipment and take other actions associated with managing commercial real estate.

The phrase "inherent authority" is sometimes used in lieu of incidental authority. For example, it is sometimes said that the authority to take an act *inheres* in a position (*e.g.*, treasurer of a firm). In any event, the concept of inherent authority is of declining importance and was dropped from the Third Restatement of Agency. It is unlikely to be of much significance in the future.

6. Delegation

Actual authority may be delegated by the agent to a subagent with the principal's consent. The only exceptions are where the agent must exercise discretion or where the agent has special skills or a special reputation. In those instances, it would not be fair to the principal to let the agent delegate his authority because the principal presumably chose the agent because of the agent's unique judgment, skill or expertise.

The principal's consent to delegation may be express or implied. A principal expressly consents to delegation by *telling* the agent that delegation is allowed.

Example #5

Principal *tells* his agent to hire an assistant. The principal has given his express consent to delegation.

Alternatively, a principal's consent may be implied from the surrounding circumstances.

Example #6

A principal hires an agent to manage his office building. The task is more than one person can reasonably handle. The principal has *impliedly* consented to the agent's hiring an assistant to help with the task because it is obvious the agent cannot accomplish the task alone.

7. *Capacity*

Because the resulting contract is between the principal and the third party, both the principal and the third party must have the *capacity* to enter a contract. The same is not true for an agent. An agent is merely an intermediary who brings the principal and third party together. Any person can do that, whether he has contractual capacity or not. For this reason, an agent does *not* have to have contractual capacity. Remember, the agent is *not* a party to the contract. The agent is merely a go-between who facilitates the formation of a contract between the principal and the third party.

B. Apparent Authority

Apparent authority arises when a principal leads a *third party* to believe an agent has authority even though the principal has never authorized the agent to perform the specific act on his behalf. The doctrine is aptly named: the principal creates the *appearance* of authority in the mind of a third party.

In a sense, apparent authority is a fiction. It is an *equitable doctrine* designed to protect a third party's *reasonable reliance* on what the principal says and does. Apparent authority hinges on whether the third party's belief is *reasonable*. Conversely, if actual authority exists, what the third party believes is irrelevant. The principal is bound by the contract.

Here is a diagram of how apparent authority operates:

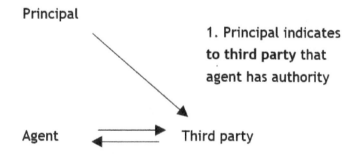

Principal

1. Principal indicates to third party that agent has authority

Agent → Third party

2. Agent contracts with third party on principals behalf

1. The principal leads the third party to believe that the agent has authority to contract on his behalf.

2. The agent executes a contract with the third party on the principal's behalf.

Result: The principal is bound to the third party on the contract. Note that the results of actual and apparent authority are *identical*.

Let us return for a moment to the real estate hypo above (Example #3). Tyra gave Vanna a minimum sales price of $300,000. Vanna sold the property for $275,000 without actual authority to do that. However, we can now see that Vanna had *apparent authority* to sell the property for that price. *Put yourself in the buyer's place.* Tyra told interested buyers *to contact Vanna.* Based on this statement, the buyer could reasonably believe that Vanna was authorized to sell the property for whatever price she could negotiate. You should always analyze apparent authority *from the perspective of a reasonable third party.*

A *secret* restriction on the minimum sales price limits only the agent's actual authority; it has no effect on apparent authority. That explains why, in the real world, a principal usually insists on signing off on a deal negotiated by an agent—to avoid the risk that the agent has "given away the shop."

As you might expect, Tyra can recover the $25,000 shortfall from Vanna for exceeding her actual authority. However, if Vanna lacks sufficient assets to reimburse Tyra, then Tyra is out of luck. Of course, Tyra could have protected herself by revealing her $300,000 bottom line to potential buyers, but if she did, she would never have been able to attract an offer for more than $300,000. That is a cardinal principle of negotiating a contract: never let the other party know your bottom line!

Keep in mind that apparent authority must be created at least in part *by the principal.* It cannot be created by the agent alone. That makes sense. We hold the principal liable because of what the *principal* did. Recall that apparent authority is an equitable doctrine based on principles of fairness. It would not be fair to hold the principal liable on the ground of apparent authority if the principal did nothing to create the impression in the mind of a third party that another person was authorized to act for the principal.

Apparent authority can be created by the principal's words or by his conduct. Things to look for when determining if an agent had apparent authority include:

— what the principal said to the third party;

— the way the principal had conducted its business in the past;

— the agent's title (for example, managing partner of the principal's firm);

— whether the principal spoke up or was silent when the agent purported to act on his behalf; and

— any prior dealings between the third party and the agent.

In determining whether apparent authority exists, courts may also take into account the way that similar businesses operate. Technically, how other businesses operate is not a representation or manifestation from the principal, so it should not be relevant to an inquiry into apparent authority. Nevertheless, if the principal's business operates in the same way other similar businesses do, that similarity may persuade a court that the third party's belief was reasonable.

1. *Simultaneous Actual and Apparent Authority*

The same conduct on the part of the principal may create *both* actual authority *and* apparent authority. In my research assistant hypo above, if my RA charges books to my bookstore account and I pay for the books without objecting to what my RA did, *both* my RA *and* the bookstore can reasonably believe that my RA is authorized to charge books to my account again. Thus, my paying for the books without raising a stink would create *implied actual authority* from my RA's vantage point and *apparent authority* from the bookstore's perspective. The significance of this point is not immediately apparent but will be become clear in our discussion of how different kinds of authority terminate below.

C. Termination of Authority

1. Principal's Revocation of Authority

Actual and apparent authority can co-exist, but apparent authority can *linger* in the mind of one or more third parties long after actual authority has been terminated. A principal can revoke an agent's actual authority simply by telling the agent not to do it again. The principal's revocation is the equivalent of the principal withdrawing his consent to the agency relationship. Be apprised, however, that if the principal terminates the agent's actual authority before the agreed-upon term of the agency relationship is up, the principal will be liable to the agent for breach of contract (just as he would be with any other contract).

Example #7

Lucy and Wood agree that Wood will be Lucy's exclusive agent for a two-year period. Six months later, Lucy finds someone else she thinks will do a better job. If Lucy terminates the contract (and Woods's authority along with it), Lucy will be liable to Wood for breach of contract.

By contrast, a principal can terminate an agent's *apparent* authority only by informing *third parties* that the agent is no longer authorized to act on the principal's behalf. As you can see, it is much harder for a principal to terminate apparent authority because apparent authority can exist in the minds of *many* third parties. As a result, a principal who creates the widespread appearance of authority faces a tough task in eradicating all apparent authority. Regardless, the burden of proof lies with the party who claims an agent had authority to act on a principal's behalf.

2. Agency "Coupled with an Interest"

There is one situation where a principal may not revoke an agent's actual authority: where the agency is *"coupled with an interest."* An agency relationship is usually created for the benefit of the principal; the principal appoints an agent to act on the principal's behalf. Occasionally, however, an agency relationship is created for the *benefit of the agent*. In that case, the agency is said to be *"coupled with an interest."* That phrase means that the agent has *his own* interest in the subject matter of the agency. In such a case, the principal may not revoke the agent's actual authority. Let me illustrate how it works. Jughead borrows money from Archie and gives Archie authority to sell his truck if he defaults on the loan. Archie has acquired an interest in the truck because he holds it as collateral for the loan. As a result, Jughead cannot revoke Archie's authority to sell the truck.

Discerning when an agency is coupled with an interest can be confusing. For example, an agent's right to be paid a fee or commission from the proceeds of sale *does not* establish an interest in the subject matter of the agency. So, if Jughead tells Archie to sell his truck in exchange for a 15% commission, Jughead may revoke Archie's authority. This agency is *not* coupled with an interest.

3. Other Ways to Terminate Actual Authority

Actual authority may terminate in ways other than the principal's revocation. As mentioned earlier, an agent can terminate actual authority by withdrawing his consent. Actual authority will also terminate at the end of the term specified in the agreement or on the occurrence of a specified event. If no term or event is specified in the agreement, actual authority will terminate after a *reasonable time* has passed. Actual authority does not last forever.

Example #8

I hire an agent to sell my house. Our agreement does not specify a time limit. The agent's authority will terminate after a reasonable time has passed. There is no bright-line test for what constitutes a reasonable time. It depends on the facts and circumstances of the particular transaction. For instance, actual authority may terminate sooner in a volatile market where prices are fluctuating wildly.

Actual authority also terminates if the subject matter of the agency is destroyed.

Example #9

I hire an agent to sell my house. If the house burns down, the agent's authority terminates because there is no house left to sell.

Finally, actual authority terminates on the death, incapacity, or bankruptcy of either the principal or the agent, unless the agency is "coupled with an interest."

Example #10

I borrow money, using my car as collateral for the loan. If I become incapacitated, my incapacity does not terminate the agency because the lender's power to sell my car was coupled with an interest. The agency was created for *the lender's* benefit.

D. Liability of the Third Party to the Principal

If the agent had authority to bind the principal to a contract, the third party will *almost* always be able to enforce it against the principal. However, there is more to this topic than you might expect. Let's examine the specifics.

1. *Relevant Terminology*

There are three types of principals: disclosed principals, partially disclosed principals, and undisclosed principals. Which type of principal is involved in a particular case depends on how much (or how little) the third party knows about (1) the principal's *existence* and (2) the principal's *identity*.

Disclosed principal: If the third party knows that the agent is acting for someone else and knows *who* that someone else is, the principal is referred to as a *disclosed principal*. The term accurately reflects that the principal's identity has been *disclosed* to the third party.

Example #11

A real estate agent makes an offer to purchase Seller's house on behalf of Gal Gadot. Ms. Godot is a disclosed principal. Seller knows who the principal is.

Partially disclosed principal: If the third party knows that the agent is acting for someone else, but does *not* know who that someone else is, the principal is called a *partially disclosed principal*. In short, the third party knows that a principal exists but does not know the principal's *identity*.

Example #12

A real estate agent makes an offer on behalf of an unnamed buyer (Ms. Gadot) to purchase Seller's house. Ms. Godot is a partially disclosed principal. Seller knows that the agent is representing *some* buyer but does not know exactly who that buyer is.

Undisclosed principal: If the third party does not even know that the agent is acting for someone else, but thinks the agent is representing himself, the principal is an *undisclosed principal*. The third party does not know about *either* the existence *or* the identity of the principal. The third party erroneously believes that the agent is acting on his own behalf.

Example #13

A real estate agent makes an offer to purchase Seller's house without telling Seller he is representing someone else (in fact, he is representing Gal Godot). Ms. Godot is an undisclosed principal. Seller believes the agent is acting on his own behalf, not on behalf someone else.

2. Significance of the Terminology

The distinction between a disclosed principal, a partially disclosed principal, and an undisclosed principal is important in determining whether the third party will be liable to the principal on the contract the agent entered on the principal's behalf.

Assuming the agent had authority (either actual or apparent) to act for the principal, the third party will be liable to a *disclosed* principal or a *partially disclosed* principal. Holding the third party liable makes sense. In each case, the third party knew the agent was acting for someone else, even if the third party did not know the principal's identity. Based on that reasoning, you would not expect a third party to be liable to an undisclosed principal—but you would be wrong!

As a general rule, a third party *is* liable to an undisclosed principal on the theory that the principal is as capable as the agent of fulfilling any obligations owed to the third party under the contract. This rule is, however, subject to an important exception.

If the agent has unusual skills, special expertise, or a singular reputation, the third party will *not* be liable to an undisclosed principal. It would not be fair to let the undisclosed principal enforce the contract against an innocent third party when the third party was bargaining for the agent's unique talents. Allowing the undisclosed principal to recover on these facts would be the equivalent of enforcing a bait-and-switch!

An illustration may help. You contract with Lady Gaga to sing at your wedding. Unbeknownst to you, Lady Gaga is acting on behalf of Butthead, who cannot sing worth a lick. When you refuse to let Butthead perform, he sues you for breach of contract. Thankfully, you are not liable to Butthead because (1) he was undisclosed (you did not know Lady Gaga was acting as his agent) and (2) Lady Gaga is a luminary. This is one of those *exceptional* cases where a third party will not be liable to an undisclosed principal. Essentially, it would be unjust to make you pay Butthead when you were counting on Lady Gaga.

E. Liability of the Agent to the Third Party

1. General Rule

The agent is an intermediary who brings the principal and third party together. As such, the agent is usually not liable to the third party on the contract, whether the principal fulfills its obligations under the contract or not. That conclusion is based on the premise that an agent is not a party to the contract.

2. Exception

The only exception to this general rule involves an agent who represents an *undisclosed principal*. If an agent is acting for an undisclosed principal, but purports to be acting on the agent's own account, the agent is considered a party to the contract and will thus be liable to the third party on the contract. In this situation, the agent, and not the principal, is treated as the real party in interest on the contract.

An agent will also be liable to a third party if the agent falsely represents to a third party that he has authority to act on behalf of a principal. This falsehood is known as a breach of the agent's "warranty of authority." It is only fair to hold the agent liable to the third party in that case because the third party does not have any rights against the principal (remember, the purported "agent" was not the principal's agent at all).

Finally, an agent will be liable to the third party for the agent's tortious conduct in connection with the formation or execution of the contract. A tortfeasor cannot avoid liability for his own tortious conduct merely by serving as an agent.

F. Liability of the Third Party to the Agent

1. General Rule

Just as the third party usually has no rights against the agent on the contract, the converse is also true. As a general rule, an agent has no rights *of his own* against the third party on the contract (he may, however, bring suit to enforce the *principal's* rights against the third party on the contract if he is authorized to do so). The rationale for insulating the third party against liability to the agent is the same as for shielding the agent against liability to the third party: the agent is merely an intermediary who is not a party to the contract, and thus has no rights of his own to assert against a third party. The contract is between the *principal* and the third party, not between the agent and the third party!

2. Exception

The situation is different when an agent has his *own* interest in the subject matter of the agency. In that case, the agent is permitted to sue the third party to assert or enforce his personal interest in the agency. Put another way, when an agency is established for the benefit of the agent rather than for the benefit of the principal (*i.e.*, when the agency is *"coupled with an interest"*), the agent has an interest in the contract to protect.

Example #14
Max borrows money from Mary and gives her the power to sell his camper if he defaults on the loan. Mary's power of agency *is* coupled with an interest because she holds the camper as collateral for a loan. Mary has her *own* interest in the camper.

Remember, however, that being paid a portion of the proceeds of sale as compensation is *not* deemed to be an interest in the agency.

Example #15
Mary agrees to sell Max's camper for a 15% commission. Mary's power of agency is *not* coupled with an interest. She has no interest in the camper to assert.

G. Duties of the Principal and the Agent

In an agency relationship, the agent and principal owe one another certain duties. Those duties are not the same.

1. Agent's Duties to the Principal

The agent owes the principal duties of *obedience, care, and loyalty*.

The duty of obedience requires an agent to follow the principal's reasonable instructions. We saw earlier that an agent is subject to the principal's control, so it should come as no surprise that the agent is obliged to follow the principal's reasonable instructions. That obligation comes with the territory.

An agent is also obligated to use due care in performing his required tasks. Due care is usually described as the degree of care that a reasonable person would exercise in a similar position. In this regard, the duty of care standard is on a sliding scale that varies with any special skill or experience an agent may have. It is safe to say that the *greater* an agent's expertise in the subject matter of the agency, the *greater* the degree of care the law will require the agent to exercise in fulfilling his duties to the principal.

Example #16

Principal hires two agents to help prepare his tax return: one is an accountant, the other is a graduate student in accounting. The accountant will be held to a higher standard of care than the graduate student because the accountant has far more expertise when it comes to tax than the graduate student has.

The duties of obedience and care are relatively straightforward. The agent's duty of loyalty is more complex and generates most of the caselaw in this area.

The duty of loyalty obligates an agent to put the principal's interests above the agent's own interests. For example, an agent cannot profit from the agency at the principal's expense (for example, by getting a kickback from a supplier) or taking advantage of ("usurping") an opportunity arising out of the agency without the first getting the principal's consent. (In the cases, agents never get permission!) In short, the agent is viewed as a **fiduciary** who must always put the principal *first*, even if doing so disadvantages the agent.

Example #17

A real estate developer hires an agent to find a property suitable for a new shopping mall. The agent finds a perfect site and buys it for himself without telling the developer. The agent later sells the property to the developer at a profit. The agent violated his duty of loyalty to the principal and must therefore turn his profit over to the developer. The agent cannot benefit at the principal's expense.

---

2. Principal's Duties to the Agent

The principal's duties to an agent are much less formidable. First, a principal must *pay* his agent the agreed-upon compensation, unless of course the agent has agreed to serve gratuitously. In that respect, the principal is treated like any other contract obligor—he must do what he promised to do.

Second, the principal is obligated to *reimburse* the agent for any costs the agent incurs in carrying out the agency. This sensible result ensures that the principal bears any expenses the agent incurs while doing the principal's bidding.

Finally, the principal has to *indemnify* the agent against any losses the agent suffers during the course of the agency. As between the principal and the agent, the principal is better placed to absorb those losses.

H. Ratification

1. Definition

The dictionary defines "ratify" to mean confirm or approve. That is a useful definition for our purposes. A party who ratifies a contract treats an agent's unauthorized act *as if* the agent had been authorized to act for him at the time of the contract. The act is given effect *as if it had been authorized at the outset*. There is one catch: ratification is permitted only if the purported agent indicated at the time of the contract that he was acting for someone else. If the agent made such a representation to a third party, the "someone else" may ratify the unauthorized contract and make it his own. Even though the agent was acting on his own accord at the time of the contract, the third party was under the impression that the agent was acting for someone else, so there is nothing unfair in allowing ratification.

2. *Ratification Is Retroactive*

Ratification is retroactive to the time of the original contract; in other words, it is just as if the ratifying party had been a party to the contract from the outset. In this regard, it is sometime said that the ratification "relates back" to the date of the contract. However, ratification is not allowed if it would harm an intervening bona fide purchaser ("bona fide" means for value, without notice of any infirmity).

Example #18

Marge, acting *without authority*, contracts to sell Homer's car for $6,000. Unaware of Marge's contract, Homer agrees to sell his car to Apu for $5,000. Obviously, Homer would like to ratify Marge's contract to get the extra $1,000, but he cannot ratify the contract because that would not be fair to Apu. This assumes Apu also did not know Marge had already sold the car. If he did know, Apu is not a bona fide purchaser and Homer could ratify Marge's sale.

3. Requirements for Ratification

There are three requirements for a ratification to be effective. First, the ratifying party must have knowledge of all the material facts. Second, the ratifying party must ratify the *entire* contract. The ratifying party cannot ratify part of a contract and disaffirm the rest. Third, because ratification is retroactive to the time of the original contract, the ratifying party must have contractual capacity not only at the time of ratification but *also* at the time the contract was formed.

Example #19

A promoter enters a lease for a corporation that has not yet been formed. After incorporation, the board passes a motion ratifying the lease. The attempted ratification is *not* effective because the corporation did not have contractual capacity when the promoter executed the lease. The corporation did not even *exist* when the lease was executed, so it obviously lacked capacity at that time!

Ratification can be **express** or can be **implied** from conduct. An example of an *express* ratification is where a corporation's board of directors passes a resolution to ratify a lease that a corporate officer executed without authority to bind the corporation.

By contrast, an *implied* ratification would arise if the corporation *knowingly* moved into the leased space without a formal board resolution ratifying the lease. Regardless of whether ratification is express or implied, the effect is the same: the ratifying party is liable on the contract just as if it had been a party to the contract *from the very beginning*.

I. Adoption

1. Overview

Even if an agent had no authority whatsoever to bind the principal at the time of the contract, and there was no effective ratification after the fact (for example, because the ratifying party did not have all the material facts), a principal may still **adopt** a contract as his own. Like ratification, adoption may be express or implied. In other respects, however, ratification and adoption are quite different.

2. Adoption Is Not Retroactive

The primary difference between ratification and adoption is that, unlike ratification, *adoption is not retroactive* to the time of the original contract. The adopting party is liable on the contract *only* from the moment of adoption *forward*. In this respect, adopting a contract is a lot like adopting a child. The adoptive parents are not responsible for what happened to the child *before* the adoption, but they *are* responsible for what happens to the child *afterwards*.

3. Contractual Capacity

Because adoption is not retroactive, it does not matter whether the adopting party had capacity at that time or not. As long as the adopting party has contractual capacity when he adopts the contract, the adoption will be effective.

Example #20

A promoter enters a lease on behalf of a corporation that has not yet been formed. After the corporation is formed, the board passes a motion *adopting* the lease. The adoption *is* effective because the corporation had capacity when it adopted the lease. It is irrelevant that the corporation lacked capacity when the lease was executed. The corporation is liable on the contract only from the moment of adoption forward. It is not liable for what happened prior to the adoption.

4. *Final Observation on Adoption*

Adoption is the ultimate *fallback* position. If everything else fails (no actual authority, no apparent authority, no effective ratification), look to see if there was an adoption. It is true that the adopting party will only be liable on the contract from the moment of adoption forward, but from a third party's perspective, being able to recover *something* from the adopting party is a whole lot better than recovering nothing at all!

PART II

General Partnership Law

CHAPTER 4

Introduction to Partnership Law

Statutes: Partnership law is a matter of state law, so there is the potential for 50 different partnership statutes. To foster uniformity among the states, the National Council of Commissioners on Uniform State Law ("NCCUSL") promulgated the Uniform Partnership Act ("the UPA") in 1914. NCCUSL's efforts were wildly successful; the UPA was adopted in every state except Louisiana (Louisiana's failure to adopt the UPA is hardly surprising since Louisiana follows French civil law).

The UPA has been revised several times to modernize the statute. The latest version was promulgated in 1997. Clarifying amendments were adopted in 2011 and 2013. For convenience, the Revised Uniform Partnership Act, as amended, is referred to as "RUPA." Thus far, 37 states have adopted RUPA in one format or another. Because few states have adopted the 2011 or 2013 amendments, citations to "RUPA" refer to RUPA (1997) (with a couple of clearly identified exceptions).

This book covers both the UPA and RUPA in part because it is easier to understand what is novel about RUPA by comparing the *revised* version of the Uniform Partnership Act to its predecessor. Of course, many of the substantive provisions are similar, even if the terminology or syntax has changed. Another reason for including the UPA is that it is discussed in many Business Associations casebooks. In any event, it cannot hurt to learn about both versions and may even provide you with a better understanding of the basic principles of partnership law.

Cases: If you are looking for a set of case briefs to help you prepare for class, this is not the book for you. Only a handful of cases are referred to by name or discussed at any length. Focusing on the key issues and relevant statutory provisions is a much better approach to mastering partnership law.

Terminology: This portion of the book examines four business associations that have confusingly similar names: general partnerships, limited liability partnerships, limited partnerships, and limited liability limited partnerships. Each of these names contains the word "partnership." However, "partnership" ordinarily signifies a *general* partnership. The other types of partnerships are referred to by their full names. This book follows that practice except when comparing a general partnership to, or distinguishing a general partnership from, one or more of the other types of partnerships.

A. Partnership Formation

1. Definition

Forming a general partnership entails far fewer formalities than forming other types of business associations. Under the UPA, a general partnership is formed when the definition of a partnership is met.

The UPA § 6 defines a partnership as "an association of two or more persons to carry on as co-owners a business for profit." This seemingly straightforward definition is deceptive, as there are five key aspects of the definition:

"An association": Students often misinterpret the term "association" as suggesting that the persons involved in the enterprise had the intent to operate as partners. In actuality even if those persons did *not* intend to form a partnership, a court may find that a partnership exists regardless of their intent. Such a partnership is sometimes referred to as an "inadvertent partnership." As one court astutely observed: "If a relationship contemplates an association of two or more persons to carry on as co-owners a business for profit, a partnership there is."

"Persons": A partnership requires two or more "persons" to be the owners of the firm. Of course, the term "person" encompasses human beings; however, "person," as defined in the UPA § 2, includes entities as well. Thus, at a minimum, a partnership may be formed by two human beings, two entities or one human being and one entity.

"To carry on": Although this clause makes it sound like a partnership is an on-going enterprise, a partnership may have a limited duration (*e.g.*, a partnership to last for two years) or be formed to accomplish a specific purpose (*e.g.*, a partnership to build a house).

"Business for profit": A partnership must involve a business as opposed to a hobby and must be established as a profit-making enterprise. Thus, you cannot have a non-profit partnership, even though you can have a non-profit corporation under state corporate law.

"Co-owners": By far the most problematic aspect of the UPA's definition of a partnership is the term "co-owners." Issues often arise in determining if a person is a "co-owner" of the business, as opposed to a partnership employee or creditor. The UPA provides some guidance on this issue, but not much. As a result, courts often look to outside factors when they need to assess co-ownership. We will first examine the provisions in the UPA that are relevant to this analysis and then turn to the judge-made factors.

2. Relevant UPA Provisions to Determine Co-Ownership

Under the UPA § 7(4), a person who has a right to share in profits is *presumed* to be a partner. Note that this presumption is not dependent upon *receiving* a share of the partnership's profits. Merely having the *right* to share in profits is sufficient to give rise to a presumption.

Although this presumption is our starting point, like all presumptions, it may be rebutted with contrary evidence. For example, someone who has a right to receive a share of profits may show that he has no right to exercise control over the business—as most co-owners do—and is therefore not a partner at all. The UPA § 7(4) recites a list of "safe harbors" under which this presumption is expressly negated. These safe harbors arise, thus rebutting the presumption, when profits were received for any of the following reasons:

— as repayment of a debt;

— as wages of an employee or rent to a landlord;

— as an annuity to a deceased partner's widow or representative;

— as interest on a loan; or

— as consideration for the sale of the good-will (reputation) of a business or other property.

However, you must keep in mind that falling within a "safe harbor" simply means that *no presumption* is drawn from having a right to share in the partnership's profits. In other words, falling within a "safe harbor" is *not* conclusive on the issue of whether a person is a partner. Other evidence may still persuade a court that the person is in fact a partner, and thus a co-owner of the business.

You need to distinguish whether the potential co-owner is sharing in profits or in *gross receipts*. What is the difference? Gross receipts or gross revenue is the total revenue a business receives from all its income sources, whereas profits are what is left after the business's expenses are deducted from its gross receipts. This distinction is important because per UPA § 7(3), sharing in gross receipts does not *of itself* create a partnership. Someone sharing in gross receipts *may* be a partner, but there is no presumption to that effect.

Example #1

A store in a shopping mall is obligated to pay ten percent of its gross receipts in rent to the landlord each month. That fact, in and of itself, does not make the landlord partners with the tenant.

The only other guidance provided by the UPA regarding whether persons are "co-owners" of a business that qualifies as a partnership is given in UPA § 7(2). Section 7(2) establishes that joint tenancy, tenancy in common, tenancy by the entireties, joint property, common property, or part ownership does not *of itself* establish a partnership, regardless of whether the co-owners share profits derived from the property or not. In other words, "persons" who own property together are not partners simply because they co-own the property.

3. *Judicial Factors in Determining Co-Ownership*

As noted above, courts will supplement their statutory analysis of ownership status by looking to many other factors they consider pertinent.

By far the most persuasive of these factors is whether a person has the *right to control* how the business in question operates. Having a right to control is second in importance only to whether a person has a right to share in profits. Simply put, courts reason that a co-owner of a business will usually have the right to control how the business operates, even if he never actually *exercises* that right. This reasoning is reminiscent of how courts analyze the relationship between an employer and an employee in an agency context: if an employer has the right to control the employee, the employee is usually considered to be a servant. For the same reasons, a court may tip the scales against an alleged partner to protect an innocent third party.

An example may be useful to illustrate this principle. Liv and Elliot start a private detective firm. Liv manages the business on a day-to-day basis. Elliot has the right to veto any business decisions he considers too risky but has never used his veto power. An unhappy client sues Liv and Elliot, claiming they are partners. Even though Elliot has never exercised control, a court may consider him to be a partner because he has veto power. Courts may tip the scales against Elliot to protect an innocent third party. On the other hand, a court could also find that Elliot's veto power was merely an act of ordinary care taken by a creditor to protect his investment in the firm, and thus conclude that he is not a partner at all.

Courts often look to other factors that may tip the scales in favor of ownership. One factor is the *name of the business*. For instance, consider a business named Sokolow Software and another business named Software Mart. Which of these businesses is more likely to be owned by Mr. Sokolow? Sokolow Software, right? For this reason, business names that include a person's name suggest that the named person is an owner of the business. Likewise, courts may look to a business's official documents, especially its tax returns and any licenses it may hold, and reason that persons named as partners in these documents are likely to be owners.

Yet another factor courts consider is whether a person made a *capital contribution* to the business. Contrary to what you might expect, a capital contribution is *not* required to be an owner. A person who contributes only services or even makes no contribution at all may still be an owner. Nevertheless, courts tend to view a capital contribution as evidence that the contributor is an owner of the firm.

As should be evident from the preceding paragraphs, there is no bright-line test for determining who is a partner/co-owner. Courts will look at *all* the surrounding facts and circumstances in assessing that issue.

4. *Additional Formation Requirements (or Lack Thereof)*

Forming a general partnership entails fewer formalities than forming other business associations. For starters, no public filing is necessary to form a general partnership. A general partnership is formed automatically upon "an association of two or more persons to carry on as co-owners a business for profit." In marked contrast, to form a limited partnership, limited liability partnership, limited liability limited partnership, limited liability company, or corporation, the organizer must submit a document to the Secretary of State for filing and pay the required fee. Those business associations come into existence only when the Secretary of State files the document.

Thus, the general partnership is the *only* type of business association that does *not* require a filing by the Secretary of State.[1] The rationale for this formal distinction is based on the extent to which the owners of a business can be held liable for the business's obligations. In every type of business association except a general partnership, some or all the owners are shielded from personal liability for the business's debts and obligations. The official filing puts the public on notice of the liability shield; the filed document is matter of public record. By contrast, partners in a general partnership are *personally liable* for all the firm's debts and obligations. Consequently, the policy concern of putting the public on notice of limited liability simply does not exist with a general partnership.

Another area in which the level of formality for general partnerships is reduced is the general partnership agreement. Incredibly, a general partnership agreement does not have to be put in writing. A general partnership agreement between or among the partners may be oral or may even be implied from the partners' conduct. As a result, when two or more co-owners go into business on a handshake without the filing of a public document or reducing the terms of their agreement to writing, they have formed a general partnership *by default*! They may not have intended to form a general partnership, but that is exactly what they have done.

5. *Forming a Partnership Under RUPA*

RUPA's approach to formation is nearly identical to the UPA's approach. The only major distinction is that RUPA makes explicit what was a matter of judicial construction under the UPA—that the parties' intent on whether they have formed a partnership is not

---

[1]   It is true that a sole proprietorship does not require a filing either. However, because a sole proprietorship is an unincorporated business that has only one owner (that is what "sole proprietorship" means), it is not technically a business *association* and is not otherwise discussed in this guide.

determinative on the issue of co-ownership: "[T]he association of two or more persons to carry on as co-owners a business for profit forms a partnership, *whether or not the persons intend to form a partnership.*" RUPA § 202(a) (emphasis added).

Disputes regarding the parties' intent about forming a general partnership usually arise when one of the parties claims that no partnership was formed to avoid liability to the other party or to avoid liability to a third-party creditor on an alleged "partnership" obligation. Courts tend to view these claims as self-serving, and if a court finds that the statutory definition of a partnership is met after it has examined all the facts, the court will conclude that a partnership has been formed regardless of any party's alleged contrary intent. However, in a notable 2020 decision, the Texas Supreme Court concluded that parties may agree that, as between themselves, no partnership will exist unless certain conditions are satisfied.

In *Energy Transfer Partners, L.P. v. Enterprise Products Partners, L.P.*, 63 Tex. Sup. Ct. J. 340 (Tex. 2020), two large energy companies were exploring a possible joint venture concerning a crude oil pipeline. Neither wanted to commit to the venture until they obtained shipping commitments from potential customers. They had an extensive written agreement that provided that no enforceable obligations would exist between the two companies until the boards of both companies approved the transaction and definitive agreements memorializing the transaction were executed by both parties. One of the energy companies then backed out and built the pipeline with another firm. The disappointed suitor claimed that a partnership had been formed, and it was therefore entitled to a share of the profits from the pipeline. The defendant countered that the conditions precedent for partnership formation had not been satisfied, so the plaintiff was not entitled to any pipeline profits.

Guided by the policy of freedom of contract, the Court sided with the defendant: "An agreement not to be partners unless certain conditions are met will ordinarily be *conclusive* on the issue of partnership formation between the parties" (emphasis added).

In effect, this holding allows parties contemplating a costly project to conduct preliminary investigations without assuming the risk of a long-term commitment. Of course, if no detailed preliminary agreement exists, as is the case with most inadvertent general partnerships, this decision is very unlikely to have any bearing on a dispute over whether the parties intended to form a general partnership.

6. *Partnership Agreement*

Even though partnership law does not require a written partnership agreement, it is usually a good idea to have one, as *Energy Transfer Partners* demonstrates. A written general partnership agreement can be used in the event of a dispute to show, for instance, that a partnership exists, what the terms of the partnership are, or whether a partner has loaned property or contributed the property to the partnership. You should also beware that in some cases, contract law's Statute of Frauds may require that the agreement be in writing for the agreement to be enforceable as, for example, where the partnership has a term lasting more than one year.

Even the act of negotiating a written agreement can be fruitful, as the process encourages participants to consider what will happen if problems develop down the road or what to do if a partner dies or wants to withdraw. The participants do not know at the outset who will ultimately want to rely on the written partnership agreement, so it is in the interest of all parties to be even-handed.

Yet it is important to keep in mind some of the reasons why partners often assume the risks associated with forgoing a written partnership agreement. Negotiating and drafting a written agreement is costly and can be time-consuming. There is also an increased risk that a participant may torpedo the deal if he gets spooked by potential pitfalls raised by the other side. Whether those reasons justify forging ahead without a written partnership agreement may depend on how risk-averse the decision-maker is.

7. *Partnership by Estoppel*

Under UPA § 16, even if no partnership was formed in fact, people may still be liable *as if* they were partners under the *partnership by estoppel* doctrine. Let me be clear: a partnership by estoppel is *not* a form of business association. Partnership by estoppel is an *equitable doctrine* designed to protect a third party who is *misled* into believing a partnership exists and relies to his detriment on that mistaken impression. One caveat: partnership by estoppel protects only contract claimants, not tort claimants. RUPA § 308 uses the term "purported partners" in lieu of "partnership by estoppel," but there is no *substantive* difference between the UPA and RUPA provisions dealing with this equitable doctrine.

Here is how it works. If you falsely represent to a third party that you are partners with someone else, and the third party relies on your representation, you are liable *as if you really were partners* with the other person. Your alleged partner, however, is liable as if he were partners with you only if he *consents* to your representation.

Example #2

Phoebe falsely tells a third party that she and Monica are partners. Monica affirms to the third party that what Phoebe said is true. Phoebe and Monica will be liable to the third party as if they were partners if the third party relies on Phoebe's statement to his detriment.

It is worth emphasizing that a person cannot become a partner by estoppel or a purported partner unless he *consents* to the representation of partnership. There is no affirmative duty to deny the truth of the representation. However, consent may be reasonably inferred from a person's conduct in some circumstances.

Example #3

Phoebe, *in Monica's presence*, tells a third party she is partners with Monica, even though it is not true. *Monica does not speak up.* If the third party relies on Phoebe's statement, Phoebe and Monica will be liable to the third party as if they were partners, Phoebe because she said they were partners and Monica because she did not deny it. To be clear, Monica is not liable simply because Phoebe said they were partners; Monica is liable because she let the third party believe that what Phoebe said was true when she could have made it clear by speaking up that Phoebe's statement was not true.

Partnership by estoppel liability can also arise where the representation of partnership is made *publicly*. In that instance, the person making the representation or the person consenting to the representation is liable to a third-party even if he is not aware of being held out as a partner *to that particular third party*. This is a sensible result: a public statement results in greater exposure to potential liability.

Example #4

Phoebe, with Monica's consent, advertises in a local newspaper that she and Monica are partners, even though they are not. Phoebe and Monica will be liable as if they were partners to a third party who relies on the advertisement, even though Phoebe and Monica did not know that the particular third party had seen the ad.

Partnership by estoppel operates in much the same way as apparent authority: it is your *fallback* position. If you encounter a problem involving partnership formation, look *first* to see if a partnership was in fact formed. If there was "an association of two or more persons to carry on as co-owners a business for profit," your inquiry is over. If not, look for third-party reliance that may be protected by partnership by estoppel principles.

Extra credit: Keep in mind that partnership by estoppel is designed to protect reliance *by third parties*. It has no application to claims between or among the alleged partners themselves. Do not make that mistake on your final exam!

B. Partnership Obligations

A partnership can only act through an agent, like one of the partners or a partnership employee. For the most part, the agency principles explored above apply to partnerships, partnership employees and the partners themselves.

1. Partnership's Tort Liability

Like any other employer, a partnership will be liable for a tort committed by one of its employees if the employee was a servant acting within the scope of employment when the employee committed the tort. For example, a partnership hires a Lyft driver to deliver documents for the firm. While making a delivery, the driver negligently injures a pedestrian. Because the driver was a servant and the accident occurred while the driver was "on the clock," the partnership will be jointly and severally liable with the driver to the injured pedestrian. Nothing unusual here.

Pursuant to the UPA § 13 and § 14 and RUPA § 305, a partnership is also liable for a partner's torts. However, analysis of a partner's tort differs in two respects from analysis of an employee's tort. First, there is no need to inquire if the partner is a servant (remember, partners are *co-owners* of the partnership). Second, a partnership will be liable if the partner committed the tort *within the ordinary course of the partnership's business*, as opposed to within the scope of the partner's employment. Thus, if a law firm partner commits malpractice while representing a client, the partnership will be liable to the client for the partner's malpractice along with the partner who was negligent.

2. *Partnership's Contract Liability*

A partnership will be liable on a contract executed by one of its employees if the employee had actual authority to bind the partnership or a substitute for actual authority. For instance, a partnership authorizes its office manager to order office supplies for the firm. The partnership is liable to a vendor for any supplies the office manager agrees to purchase for the firm. This example involves a straightforward application of the principles laid out in the chapter on agency law.

Partnership liability on a contract made by a partner for the partnership is a bit more complicated. Whether a partner has authority to bind the partnership on a contract is governed by the general partnership statute. Fortunately, the UPA § 9 and RUPA § 301 embody the common law principles of actual and apparent authority. These statutes make every partner an agent of the partnership for the purpose of its business. Thus, every partner has *actual* authority to bind the partnership.

However, this statutory actual authority is not absolute; partners can limit, or even eliminate, a partner's actual authority to bind the partnership, by agreement among themselves.

Example #5

Moe, Larry and Curly are partners. They agree that only Moe will have authority to buy inventory for the firm. Pursuant to that agreement, Larry and Curly have relinquished their actual authority to buy inventory on the partnership's behalf.

The UPA § 9 and RUPA § 301 also recognize the concept of apparent authority. A partnership will be bound if a partner's act is for *apparently* carrying on the partnership's business in the usual way, unless the partner lacked actual authority to bind the partnership *and* third party with whom the partner was dealing knew that the partner had no such authority. This limitation makes sense: if a third party *knows* a partner does not have actual authority to bind the partnership, the third party cannot reasonably believe the partner had actual authority to bind the partnership to him.

3. *Statement of Partnership Authority*

RUPA § 303 permits a partnership to protect itself against potential third-party claims by submitting to the Secretary of State for filing a document known as a Statement of Partnership Authority. Although a partnership is not required to file such a Statement, a partnership may choose to do so to put the public on notice of the partners' authority, or lack of authority, to bind the partnership.

A Statement of Partnership Authority can help a partnership defend against a breach of contract claim if the Statement says the partner has no authority to do what he did (of course, it works against the partnership if the Statement says the partner *did* have authority). A Statement of Partnership Authority is good for five years from the date it is filed.

Unfortunately for the partnership, a limitation on a partner's authority in a Statement of Partnership Authority will not protect the partnership against third-party claims very often. Any such limitation is effective *only* against a third party who *knew* about it. Since most third parties will not check with the Secretary of State to see if the partnership has filed a Statement of Partnership Authority, the Statement will not do the partnership much good.

The only exception entails a partner's transferring to a third-party *real property held in the partnership's name*. In that instance, the buyer is *deemed* to know of the limitation if the Statement of Partnership Authority is *also* filed in the recording office of the county where the real property is located. Why does the third party have *constructive knowledge* here but not in other transactions? The law expects that someone who is purchasing real property will check with the relevant county recording office to see if there is any cloud on the title, like a tax lien or a mechanic's lien on the property. If the buyer checks, he will discover the Statement of Partnership Authority; if he does not, he is charged with *constructive knowledge of its contents* anyway. The bottom line: A Statement of Partnership Authority is of limited utility from the partnership's perspective.

4. Statement of Denial

A partner named in a Statement of Partnership Authority may submit a Statement of Denial to the Secretary of State for filing denying his authority to bind the partnership or even denying the fact that he is a partner at all. A filed Statement of Denial operates as a limitation on the person's authority to bind the partnership; it negates a grant of authority contained in a Statement of Partnership Authority. FYI, Statements of Denial are rarely used in practice.

C. Managing the Partnership

When it comes to managing partnership affairs, the statutory default rule envisions a decentralized management structure in which (1) all partners have *equal* rights in management and control of the firm and (2) any disagreement about matters of ordinary business are decided by a majority of the partners. However, partners are free to allocate control over partnership affairs however they see fit by agreement among themselves.

While matters of ordinary business are decided by a majority vote of the partners, certain issues are considered so important that the statute requires *unanimous consent* to vary from the default rule. One such issue involves the decision to add a new partner to an existing partnership; another concerns taking an action that violates the partnership agreement. In each of those cases, unanimity is required unless the partners have agreed that a lesser vote is sufficient to add a new partner or to act in a manner contrary to the partnership agreement. Imagine a partnership with 99 partners. Ninety-eight vote in favor of admitting Lebron as a partner; the one partner who is a Clippers fan votes against admitting Lebron. Despite the overwhelming support from the partners, Lebron has *not* been admitted to the partnership under the default rule.

Disagreements concerning matters of ordinary business can be problematic where there are only two partners. What if the two partners disagree about how to run the partnership business on a day-to-day basis? Courts have reached seemingly inconsistent results.

One line of cases says that one equal partner cannot deprive the other equal partner of his statutory authority. These cases aim to protect a partner's autonomy. Another line of cases says that in the event of a disagreement, where partners are equally divided, those who forbid change must prevail. These cases preserve the status quo.

One factor a court may consider in resolving this issue is the plaintiff's relationship to the partnership. Is the plaintiff a *third party* trying to hold the partnership liable on an obligation arising from one partner's acting contrary to the other's instructions or is the plaintiff a *partner* attempting to get contribution from the other partner? A court may be more inclined to rule in favor of a third-party plaintiff and let partners who are embroiled in a dispute fend for themselves.

D. Partners' Liability to Third Parties

1. Overview

We saw earlier that a partnership is an association of two or more persons. Under the *aggregate* theory of partnerships adopted by the UPA, a partnership is not an entity that is separate and distinct from the partners. It is a collection (or aggregation) of persons. In a sense, the partners and the partnership are one and the same. It thus follows that the liability of a partner and the liability of the partnership are closely intertwined.

Under UPA § 9(1), partners are considered agents of the partnership for the purpose of its business. As a result, the partnership can be held liable for the act of a single partner. Conversely, under UPA § 15, a partner is personally liable for partnership obligations. The result for law students: a liability nightmare!

If a partnership obligation results from the act of one of its agents, the partnership is liable for the obligation. Fair enough. Unfortunately, the primary downside of doing business as a general partnership is that not only is the partnership liable, but the partners are *personally liable* for partnership obligations, *too*! That is a sobering fact: *every* partner is liable for *all* partnership obligations even if he was not involved in the conduct giving rise to the obligation.

Here is a scary example. You join a law firm general partnership. One of your partners commits malpractice while representing a client in court. Although you were not involved in the matter, you are nonetheless liable to the client for its damages—*all* its damages! The practical lesson of this example should be clear: *do not operate a business as a general partnership in the real world!* The risk of personal liability is simply too great.

2. Liability Under the UPA

Under the UPA, a plaintiff may sue the partnership to recover for a partnership obligation or may proceed directly against the partners without having to sue the partnership first. Whether a plaintiff must sue all the partners or may sue merely some partners or just one partner depends on whether the liability arises from a tort or a contract obligation.

Tort liability: A partnership—and thereby the partners—can be held liable not only for torts committed by its *employees* in the course and the scope of their employment, but also for torts committed by *partners* acting in the ordinary course of the partnership's business. Under UPA § 15(a), partners are *jointly and severally liable for partnership torts*. Joint and several liability permits a plaintiff to sue *any partner(s)* for the full obligation (several liability) or to join *all* the partners as defendants (joint liability).

Contract liability: Recall from our discussion of agency law that a principal (here, the partnership) is liable for a contract entered into by an agent (here, a partner) acting with actual or apparent authority. Under UPA § 15(b), partners are *jointly liable* *on partnership contracts*, not jointly and severally liable as they are on tort obligations.

The distinction between joint liability and joint and several liability is *procedural* in nature. Joint liability requires a plaintiff to join *all* the partners as defendants to recover from the partners personally. If a plaintiff is unable to join all the partners as defendants (for example, because he lacks jurisdiction over one of the partners), the plaintiff will not be able to recover from the partners. His only option would be to go against the partnership.

By making partners jointly and severally liable for partnership torts, but only jointly liable on partnership contracts, the UPA evidences a bias in favor of tort claimants, perhaps because contract claimants can protect themselves against possible losses in advance. For example, a potential supplier or lender to the partnership can negotiate for a *personal guarantee* from a partner or a *security interest* in the partnership's assets *before* committing to sell goods on credit or loan money to the partnership. Most tort claimants do not have the luxury of protecting themselves upfront. Accordingly, they are afforded special treatment under the UPA when it comes to holding partners accountable.

3. *Liability Under RUPA*

There are two major differences between the way the UPA and RUPA approach liability to third parties. First, in contrast to the UPA § 15, RUPA § 306(a) makes partners jointly and severally liable for *all* partnership obligations, regardless of whether they arise in contract or in tort.

Second, RUPA imposes an **"exhaustion requirement."** Under RUPA § 307(d), a partnership creditor must first *exhaust partnership resources* before it can pursue a partner's personal assets. If the claimant cannot demonstrate to the court's satisfaction that the partnership's resources are insufficient to cover the obligation, then the claimant cannot recover from individual partners on the partnership obligation. In this regard, RUPA makes partners *guarantors* of partnership obligations rather than principal debtors. There is no exhaustion requirement under the UPA.

Example #6

Citibank loans the AB Partnership $50,000. The partnership defaults on the loan. Citibank sues A and B jointly to recover the balance due on the loan. Citibank cannot recover from A and B personally unless it demonstrates to the court that the partnership lacks sufficient assets to pay off the loan.

The exhaustion requirement may be explained in part by RUPA's adoption of an *entity* theory of partnerships. Under RUPA § 201, "a partnership is an entity distinct from its partners." Consistent with this premise, RUPA replaces the UPA's "free-for-all" approach to liability on a partnership obligation with a "partnership first, partners second" liability schema. The partners are still personally liable for partnership obligations, but only if the partnership's well has run dry.

4. *Incoming Partner*

We should also note that a person who joins an existing partnership (sometimes called an **"incoming partner"**) will not be *personally* liable to third-party creditors for any partnership obligations that arose *before* he joined the partnership.

The rules addressing the liability of an incoming partner in UPA § 17 and RUPA § 306(b) are substantially the same. An incoming partner may lose whatever capital he contributed to the partnership as well as his share of the partnership's profits, but he will *not* have to reach into his pocket to pay off a third-party creditor. In that respect, the statute cuts an incoming partner some slack because he was not a member of the partnership when the obligation was originally incurred. However, with respect to any *subsequent* obligations, an incoming partner will be liable to third parties just like all the other partners. There is no reason to cut an incoming partner slack on debts incurred *after* he becomes a partner.

5. *Indemnification and Contribution*

Under UPA § 18(a), partners can agree to apportion responsibility for the partnership's losses among themselves in any manner they wish. However, that apportionment agreement is *not* effective against third parties. Partners cannot limit a third party's rights without that third party's consent. If they could limit a third party's rights, partners would simply agree that none of them was liable and thereby insulate themselves from liability to third parties on partnership obligations. So, think of it this way: the partnership agreement on how losses will be shared is effective as an *indemnification or contribution agreement* among the partners themselves and/or the partnership, but it will have no effect on the rights of third parties to hold partners personally liable for partnership obligations.

If a partner lays out money on the partnership's behalf or is held liable to a third party on a partnership obligation, the partner is entitled to be reimbursed by the partnership and by the other partners. Be sure to take note of the proper terminology for these different kinds of "payback": a partnership *indemnifies* a partner for the money he is out of pocket while other partners *contribute* their pro rata share of whatever the partner expended.

Example #7

Partner A pays off a $50,000 partnership obligation. A is entitled to be indemnified by the partnership and to get contribution from the other partners for their pro rata share of the $50,000.

However, if the partnership and/or the other partners do not have sufficient assets to reimburse the partner for the obligation, the partner who paid out the money is left "holding the bag." This is the primary reason why one should avoid operating a business as a general partnership: every partner's personal assets are (and his ass is) on the line!

Example #8

Same facts as in Example #7. The partnership and the other partners are insolvent. Partner A must bear the entire $50,000 expenditure.

E. Property Interests in a Partnership

1. Partnership Property

How can you tell if property is owned by the partnership or is owned by someone else and merely on loan to the partnership? There are only two provisions in the UPA addressing this issue and neither provides much clarity.

UPA § 8(2) states: "Unless the contrary intention appears, property acquired with partnership funds is partnership property."

Any certainty this rule-of-thumb provides is undercut by the initial clause. A court must undertake a fact-specific inquiry to determine whether a contrary intention appears. An illustration may help. A partnership buys a car on the partnership's line of credit. Based on that fact alone, the car is presumed to belong to the partnership. (Yes, the term "funds" includes credit as well as money.) However, a court will have to consider contrary evidence that the partnership bought the car as bonus compensation for its top-producing salesperson. We cannot tell in the abstract if the car belongs to the partnership or the salesperson.

The companion provision in UPA § 8(1) also fosters uncertainty: "All property brought into the partnership stock or subsequently acquired by purchase or otherwise, on account of the partnership, is partnership property." In contemporary terms, "brought into the partnership stock" means something like "conveyed to the partnership as a capital contribution." Regardless of the phraseology, the critical question is: how do you know if property was "brought into the partnership stock" or "acquired . . . on account of the partnership"? The answer depends on the *intent* of the partners. Once again, a court must examine all the facts to ascertain whether property has become partnership property or not.

Courts look to a variety of factors in determining intent. Many of the factors relate to the usual attributes of ownership, like use, upkeep, and title. Here are some of the factors courts often address in trying to ascertain whether property belongs to the partnership or to someone else:

Evidence: Is there evidence a partner contributed the property to the partnership? Conversely, is there evidence a partner was simply loaning the property to the partnership? (Written evidence is particularly useful in answering these questions.)

Use: Is the partnership using the property in its business? If so, how frequent or extensive is the partnership's use of the property?

Upkeep: Does the partnership pay to insure and maintain the property or are those costs borne by one someone else?

Title: Is title to the property held in the partnership's name or in the name of another person?

You might assume that title is conclusive as to who owns the property, but you would be *wrong*! Of course, partnership property *may* be held in the name of the partnership, but it does not have to be. Under UPA § 10, partnership property may be held in the name of one, or some, or all the partners, or even in the name of a third-party nominee. As a result, the name in which title to property is held is *not* conclusive about who owns the property. Title to property may not be held in the partnership's name and yet the property may belong to the partnership. The converse is true as well.

In contrast to the UPA, RUPA sets forth rules in § 204 to determine when property—real or personal—belongs to a partnership. Having a set of rules fosters certainty, which is particularly important if a transfer of real property is involved. Unlike the UPA, RUPA emphasizes *record title*. Here are the rules, quoted mostly verbatim followed by a brief explanation of each rule:

Rule #1: Property is partnership property "if acquired in the name of the partnership."

Rule #2: Property is partnership property "if acquired in the name of one or more partners with an indication in the instrument passing title to the property of the person's capacity as a partner or of the existence of a partnership but without an indication of the name of the partnership."

Rule #3: Property is presumed to be partnership property "if purchased with partnership assets."

Rule #4: Property is presumed to be separate property of a partner "if acquired in the name of one or more partners, without an indication in the instrument passing title to the property of the person's capacity as a partner or of the existence of a partnership and without the use of partnership assets."

If Rule #1 or Rule #2 is satisfied, the property belongs to the partnership. Period. Evidence of intent is irrelevant. By contrast, Rule #3 and Rule #4 give rise to *presumptions* about who owns the property. However, these presumptions may be rebutted, so evidence of intent still matters when it comes to applying Rule #3 and Rule #4.

Rule #1 permits a partnership to eliminate any doubt about ownership by putting title in the partnership's name. If a partner transfers to a third party property held in the partnership's name, the partnership may recover the property if there is a limitation on the partner's authority to transfer the property in a duly-filed Statement of Partnership Authority (discussed above under "Partnership Obligations").

Rule #2 is admittedly confusing but makes sense on further examination. We can sort through it here. If a partner buys property in his own name, but the title document indicates that the partner is acting for a partnership, then the property belongs to the partnership even though the partnership is not specifically mentioned in the document by name. In other words, if the title document indicates that a person is acting in a representative capacity—as an agent for a partnership—the property belongs to the principal, *i.e.*, the partnership. That result is consistent with the agency principles explored above.

Rule #3 is common sense. If you use *your own* assets to acquire property, the property most likely belongs to *you*. The same reasoning applies where the partnership furnishes the assets. If partnership assets are used to purchase property, the property is *presumed* to belong to the partnership. The term "assets" includes the partnership's credit as well as cash and other property.

Rule #4 is a "catchall": if none of the first three rules applies the property is *presumed* to belong to the partner in whose name the property was acquired. It is easy to see why. If the property was acquired in the partner's name, there was no indication in the title document he was acting for a partnership, and partnership assets were not used, then it looks like the partner bought the property for himself. The fact that the partnership is using the property does not change things. Presumably, the partner who owns the property loaned it to the partnership. Remember, however, that this presumption may be rebutted by other contrary evidence.

2. A Partner's Rights in Partnership Property

Partnership property does not belong to the partners; it belongs to the partnership. The partnership can do whatever it wants to with partnership property because the partnership owns the property. No surprise there. But what can *partners* do with property that belongs to the partnership? The UPA § 25(1) makes partners "tenants in partnership" with respect to partnership property, but that designation is misleading. The phrase "tenancy in partnership" makes it sound like partners have an ownership interest in partnership property, but that is not the case.

A partner's rights in partnership property are *extremely* limited. Under UPA § 25(2), the *only* thing a partner may do with partnership property is use it *for partnership purposes* unless he gets consent from partnership (pursuant to a vote of the other partners). A partner may not assign, devise, or otherwise transfer his rights in partnership property because he has *no rights in partnership property to convey*. Similarly, a partner's creditors may not attach his interest in partnership property *because he has no interest in the property to attach*. That makes sense: you cannot use or convey someone else's property without first getting the owner's consent. So, too, a partner cannot use or convey the partnership's property without first getting the *partnership's* consent.

A simple example should suffice. A partnership owns a truck. The partnership may pledge the truck as collateral for a loan to the partnership, but a partner may not pledge his interest in the truck as collateral for a personal loan because he has no interest in the truck to pledge. Similarly, a partnership creditor may attach the truck to recover on a partnership obligation, but a partner's individual creditor may not attach the truck to recover on the partner's personal obligation because he has no interest in the truck to attach.

As is so often the case, RUPA reaches the same result but in a more comprehensible fashion. RUPA § 501 dispenses with the notion of tenancy in partnership and makes it crystal clear: "A partner is *not* a co-owner of partnership property and has no interest in [it] that can be transferred, either voluntarily or involuntarily" (emphasis added). There is no ambiguity here.

3. *A Partner's Economic Interest in the Partnership*

A partner's economic interest in the partnership encompasses the partner's share of profits and his right to receive distributions from the partnership. Thus, a partner who is entitled to receive 25% of the partnership's profits has a 25% interest (financial stake) in the partnership.

Under both the UPA and RUPA, a partner's economic interest in the partnership is freely transferable, just like any other financial asset. In fact, under RUPA § 102, it is referred to as a "partner's transferable interest" in the partnership.

However, the transfer of a partner's economic interest in the partnership *does not* entitle the transferee to participate in the conduct of the partnership's business, to get access to information about partnership transactions, to inspect or copy partnership books and records, or to become a partner. All the transfer does is redirect to the transferee distributions that would otherwise have gone to the transferor. In essence, the partnership writes a check to the transferee instead of to the transferor partner. Transfer of a partner's economic interest *does not* cause dissolution of the partnership or initiate the winding up of partnership affairs.

A partner's *judgment creditor* may attach the partner's economic interest in the partnership by getting a "**charging order**" from a court. A charging order pays off the judgment by allowing the judgment creditor to receive any distribution that would otherwise have been made to the debtor partner. However, the charging order does not make the partner's judgment creditor a partner or convey to the partner's judgment creditor any right to participate in partnership affairs. To clarify: a charging order is available *only* to a creditor who has secured a *judgment* against a partner, *not* to a partner's *other* creditors.

If the charging order will not pay off the debt within a reasonable time, the judgment creditor may purchase the partner's interest in the partnership at a foreclosure sale and ask a court to dissolve the partnership. On dissolution, the judgment creditor would receive the value of the debtor-partner's interest in the partnership.

In community property states, a partner's economic interest in a partnership is treated like any other financial asset. If the interest was acquired during the life of the community, it is considered community property.

When a partnership ends, if partnership assets are not sufficient to cover its obligations, creditors of the partnership may have to compete with the partners' separate creditors for a share of the partnership's assets and a share of the partners' personal assets. Under the UPA § 40, partnership creditors have priority on partnership assets while a partner's separate creditors have priority on the partner's separate assets. These dual priorities are sometimes referred to as the "jingle rule."

Under RUPA, partnership creditors still have priority on partnership property, but the statute is silent on who has priority on a partner's separate property. RUPA leaves that issue to federal bankruptcy law, which treats *all* creditors on a par when it comes to a partner's separate assets. The rationale for this approach is that partnership creditors rely on the partners' separate assets as well as partnership assets in deciding whether to lend money or sell on credit to the partnership, so they should have *equal* rights with separate creditors when it come to the partners' separate assets. As a result, partnership creditors usually bring suit in federal court to take advantage of the bankruptcy code's favorable treatment.

F. Duties of Partners

1. *The Original Paradigm: Meinhard v. Salmon*

Traditionally, partners were viewed as fiduciaries who owed a duty of loyalty to the partnership. It is only a slight exaggeration to say that courts viewed this duty as sacred. *Meinhard v. Salmon*, 249 N.Y. 458 (1928), written by Judge Benjamin Cardozo, set an extraordinarily high standard for partners to maintain. Because *Meinhard* is the most frequently-cited case in all of partnership law, it merits a closer look. A word of warning: if a court cites *Meinhard v. Salmon*, the defendant is going to lose!

Salmon entered a twenty-year lease for the Bristol Hotel, then formed a joint venture with Meinhard for a twenty-year term, coextensive with the lease (a joint venture is treated just like a partnership). Meinhard was to contribute half the funds necessary to renovate the property. Salmon had the sole right to manage and operate the hotel. Several months before the lease expired, the owner of the hotel property approached Salmon, who appeared to hold the lease for himself alone, about leasing the Bristol Hotel property and five adjacent lots for another twenty years. Salmon's corporation signed a new lease on the entire parcel, but Salmon did not tell Meinhard. When Meinhard found out about the opportunity, he offered to share the risk of the new venture with Salmon. Salmon refused to let Meinhard participate.

Meinhard sued Salmon for breaching his duty of loyalty to the partnership by *usurping* (taking advantage of) a partnership opportunity. He claimed the new lease should have been exploited for the *partnership's* benefit, not for Salmon's benefit alone.

Cardozo measured Salmon's conduct against a trustee's duty to the beneficiary of a trust: "Not honesty alone, but the punctilio of an honor the most sensitive" is required. Judged by this standard, Salmon failed miserably. Not surprisingly, the court held Salmon liable for breaching his fiduciary to duty to the partnership and to his partner, Meinhard.

A close reading of *Meinhard* provides a roadmap for analyzing a *partnership opportunity* case. There are six significant considerations to address: (1) the nexus between the partnership and the opportunity; (2) disclosure of the opportunity to the other partner(s); (3) the partnership's ability to take advantage of the opportunity had the opportunity been disclosed; (4) the defendant's timing in exploiting the opportunity; (5) the plaintiff's timing in bringing the lawsuit; and (6) an appropriate remedy.

Nexus: Was there a partnership opportunity to usurp? For a partnership opportunity to exist, there must be a *nexus* (the Latin word for "connection") between the existing partnership and the opportunity. Without this nexus, there is no partnership opportunity to usurp.

Cardozo found a nexus in *Meinhard* because (1) the same piece of property was involved in both ventures, and (2) the owner offered the new lease to Salmon because he appeared to be the sole holder of the existing lease (Meinhard was a silent partner). Presumably, if the owner had known that Salmon and Meinhard were partners in the Bristol Hotel lease, he would have approached them both with the opportunity. Judge Cardozo pretermits the question of whether there would have been a nexus if the opportunity involved a piece of property across town, but it is possible a partnership opportunity could still exist in that case if there were other facts linking the opportunity to the original venture.

A nexus may also exist if the opportunity involves the same kind of business as the partnership or if there are other connections between the original partnership and the opportunity. A written partnership agreement, if there is one, can often play a critical role in determining whether a nexus exists. For example, does the language of the partnership agreement suggest that the partnership was formed to drill a single oil well or to engage in a variety of drilling activities? Obviously, the broader the scope of business described in the written partnership agreement, the more likely it is that a court will find the requisite nexus between the partnership and the later opportunity.

Alternatively, if an agreement is ambiguous about how extensive the original partnership's business was intended to be, a court may rely on a "sniff test" to determine whether a partnership opportunity was usurped. The lesson of this cautionary tale is clear: draft partnership agreements carefully to avoid the prospect of a partnership opportunity claim!

Disclosure: Did the defendant partner disclose the existence of the opportunity to the other partner(s)? Cardozo was troubled by Salmon's failure to disclose the opportunity to Meinhard. Had Salmon disclosed the opportunity to lease the Bristol Hotel property and adjacent lots, Meinhard could have competed with Salmon for the new lease on an even playing field. Cardozo does not say that disclosure would have let Salmon off the hook (pun intended) but it might have affected the result in *Meinhard*, which was a 4-3 decision in favor of the plaintiff. Nonetheless, the truth is that in the real world, usurping partners *never* disclose that an opportunity exists; they sneak around behind the other partners' backs to secure an unjust reward. Thus, you are unlikely to encounter a forthright defendant in a partnership opportunity case no matter how many years you practice partnership law.

Partnership's resources: Could the partnership or the other partners have exploited the opportunity if the existence of the opportunity had been disclosed by the defendant? Cardozo dismisses this question as mere conjecture because Salmon did not disclose the opportunity before taking advantage of it. Other courts may be more receptive to the argument that the partnership lacked the resources to take advantage of the opportunity, reasoning that even if the existence of the opportunity *had* been disclosed, the partnership would not have been able to exploit it. The rationale supporting this approach can be succinctly characterized as, "No harm, no foul!"

Defendant's timing: When did the *defendant* take advantage of the opportunity? A partner who learns of the opportunity during the life of the partnership cannot wait until the partnership is over to appropriate a partnership opportunity and thereby avoid liability for breach of fiduciary duty. That is common sense: you cannot escape your fiduciary duty merely by stalling.

Plaintiff's timing: When did the *plaintiff* assert an interest in the opportunity? Partners often wait to see whether an opportunity pans out before asserting a partnership opportunity claim; yet courts rarely deny them relief on that basis. Here, the plaintiff gets the benefit of hindsight. As between the defendant's breach of fiduciary duty and the plaintiff's delay in bringing a claim, courts view the delay as the lesser of two evils. The fact that a partner waited to assert his claim is unlikely to be fatal to that claim.

Remedy: An appropriate remedy should ensure that profits from the new venture are divided up in the same way they would have been if the opportunity had been exploited by the partnership rather than the defendant partner. (For more details, see section 6. below.) To this end, Cardozo basically awarded Meinhard a fifty percent interest in the corporation Salmon had formed to capitalize on the opportunity, so that Meinhard would receive half the profits from the new venture, just as he would have had the Meinhard-Salmon partnership been able to avail itself of the new deal.

One last thought about partnership opportunities. It may be obvious, but it is worth noting: if the opportunity generates a *loss* rather than the anticipated profit, the partner who usurped the opportunity cannot recover from other partners for their share of the loss. Courts will not allow the disloyal partner to "hedge his bets" in this fashion. Thus, partnership opportunity jurisprudence can be summed up in the phrase: "Heads I [the plaintiff] win, tails you [the defendant] lose." Do not expect to get the court's sympathy if you usurp a partnership opportunity!

2. *Fiduciary Duties Under the UPA*

Today, we tend to think of fiduciary duties in terms of a "duty of loyalty" and "duty of care." However, the drafters of the UPA adopted a more amorphous approach.

Under the heading "Partner Accountable as a Fiduciary," UPA § 19 provides that "Every partner must account to the partnership for any benefit, and hold *as trustee* for it any profits derived by him without the consent of the other partners from any transaction connected with the formation, conduct, or liquidation of the partnership or from any use by him of its property" (emphasis added). Courts construed this provision to embody the principles espoused in the *Meinhard* case. That is not surprising, given the reference to "fiduciary" in the heading and the designation of a partner as a "trustee" in the body of the statute. Consistent with *Meinhard*'s strict approach to fiduciary duty, most courts routinely rebuffed attempts by partners to "contract away" liability for breach of fiduciary duty in a partnership agreement.

The UPA did not impose a duty of care on the partners. Nor was a duty of care imposed by the courts. The *only* fiduciary duty partners owed to the partnership and to one another was what we would characterize today as a duty of loyalty.

3. *Fiduciary Duties Under RUPA (1997)*

When the UPA was extensively revised in 1997, the drafters adopted more modern terminology. They couched a partner's fiduciary duties in terms of a "duty of care" and a "duty of loyalty."

The duty of care embodied in RUPA (1997) § 404(c) is essentially the same duty of care to which corporate directors are held: a partner must refrain from engaging in "grossly negligent or reckless conduct, intentional misconduct, or a knowing violation of the law." This standard mirrors the so-called Business Judgment Rule that shields corporate directors from personal liability for business decisions if they used due care in the decision-making process. Partners will not be liable to the partnership for making a decision that works out badly for the partnership if they made an informed decision. Basically, if the partners "did their homework," they used due care. You cannot use hindsight to judge them because "hindsight is 20/20," as they say.

The most significant change wrought by RUPA with regard to a partner's fiduciary duties was a retreat from the strict *Meinhard* standard. The drafters took several steps to achieve this result in Section 404.

First, they made it clear that "[t]he *only* fiduciary duties a partner owes to the partnership and the other partners are the duty of loyalty and the duty of care" as defined in the statute (emphasis added).

Second, they were careful to limit the scope of these duties. The duty of care was "*limited to* refraining from engaging in grossly negligent or reckless conduct, intentional misconduct, or a knowing violation of law" (emphasis added). The duty of loyalty was likewise "*limited to*" certain kinds of conduct, including the appropriation of a partnership opportunity.

Finally, RUPA (1997) eliminated a partner's duty of loyalty in connection with partnership *formation* on the theory that parties should be free to negotiate at arm's length before a partnership has been formed. The net effect of all these changes was to reduce the prospect of a partner's liability for breach of fiduciary duty under RUPA (1997).

The more restrictive tack regarding fiduciary duties adopted by RUPA (1997) did not meet with universal approval. For example, some states that adopted RUPA (1997) declined to adopt the statute's provisions on fiduciary duties, preferring to maintain the traditional *Meinhard*/UPA approach to fiduciary duties. *Meinhard* was so deeply ingrained in partnership jurisprudence, it was difficult for some states to let the case go.

In another break with traditional partnership jurisprudence, RUPA (1997) allows partners to limit their fiduciary duties by agreement among themselves. While RUPA (1997) § 103(b) does not permit partners to *eliminate* the duty of loyalty or the duty of care, it allows partners to reduce the standards prescribed in the statute within reasonable limits. In other words, partners can *tinker* with the duties of care and loyalty as long as the "tinkering" is reasonable but cannot eliminate them entirely.

Some states go even further. Delaware, for example, permits partners to eliminate *both* the duty of care and the duty of loyalty. Texas allows partners to eliminate *only* the duty of care. Given the variation among state partnership statutes, you should check to see which approach your state follows.

4. *Fiduciary Duties Under RUPA (2013)*

As noted above, some states that adopted RUPA (1997) refused to adopt its restrictive provisions on fiduciary duties. Perhaps for this reason, the drafters backpedaled in this area when they made amendments to RUPA in 2013. They "uncabined" (loosened up) partners' fiduciary duties by removing the words "only" and "limited" from the statute. As a result, it is harder to predict under RUPA (2013) whether a partner's conduct constitutes a breach of his fiduciary duties than it was under RUPA (1997). It is likely that the drafters of RUPA (2013) believed that the costs associated with this additional level of uncertainty were outweighed by the benefits of allowing courts more latitude in deciding whether a partner's conduct amounted to a breach of fiduciary duty.

RUPA (2013) goes one step beyond RUPA (1997) when it comes to contracting around partners' fiduciary duties. Under RUPA (2013), if it is not manifestly unreasonable, a partnership agreement may (1) alter *or eliminate* the duty of loyalty; (2) alter the duty of care, but may not authorize conduct involving bad faith, willful or intentional misconduct, or knowing violation of the law; (3) alter *or eliminate* any other fiduciary duties. Because the rights of third parties are not affected, RUPA (2013) affords partners considerable leeway in this area.

5. *Discovering a Breach of Fiduciary Duty*

How can you tell if a partner has breached his fiduciary duties to the partnership? One option is to inspect the partnership's books and records, which every partner has the right to do under the UPA § 19 and RUPA § 403(b). An irregularity may reveal that a partner did something inappropriate.

Another option is simply asking a partner what he has done. Under the UPA § 20, a partner is required to disclose information about the partnership only if a *demand* for the information is made. RUPA handles this issue a bit differently. RUPA § 403(c) imposes an affirmative duty to disclose information that a partner needs to exercise his rights under the partnership agreement or under the statute, regardless of whether a demand is made or not. In contrast, a partner does not have to disclose any *other* information unless a demand is made. This bifurcated demand requirement facilitates a partner's getting the information he needs to make an informed decision.

6. *Remedy for Breach of Fiduciary Duty*

Under UPA, RUPA (1997) and RUPA (2013), a partner who discovers a breach may ask the court to order an accounting of who owes what to whom. The partners who breach their fiduciary duties must disgorge to the partnership any benefit improperly derived from their breach.

To protect the partnership and the partners who were harmed by the breach, a court may impose an equitable remedy known as a *constructive trust*. As the term "constructive" implies, a constructive trust is a fiction; no actual (express) trust is established. Instead, the court treats property improperly acquired by a partner *as if* the property had been placed in a trust created for the benefit of the partnership. That way, the resulting benefit accrues *to the partnership* and thus *to all the partners*, not just to the breaching partner. Constructive trusts are often imposed in partnership opportunity cases, like *Meinhard*, where a partner tries to appropriate for himself property or some other benefit that should have been made available to the partnership.

7.　*Suing the Partnership or Another Partner*

Courts held that a partner could not bring a lawsuit against the partnership or another partner on a partnership matter under the UPA without first dissolving the partnership, even though the UPA was silent on this matter. Bringing a lawsuit during the life of the partnership was viewed as being too disruptive to the partnership's business to be allowed.

RUPA addresses this issue head on and states a markedly different rule. Under RUPA § 405, a partner may bring a lawsuit against the partnership or another partner on a partnership matter without dissolving or terminating the partnership. The statute of limitations for such a suit begins to run when a partner's claim against the partnership and/or other partners accrues, so if a partner does not bring a timely lawsuit on the claim, he risks that the statute of limitations will run on the claim before he initiates a cause of action. Apparently, the drafters of RUPA assume that partners can handle the fallout from a partner's claim against the partnership or against the other partners even though they are still in business together.

G.　**Sharing Profits and Losses**

1.　*Sharing Profits*

In the absence of an agreement to the contrary, under the UPA § 18(a) and RUPA § 401(b), partners split profits *equally*. This arrangement may not be appropriate in every situation. For example, if a business is capital-intensive, the partner who contributes the lion's share of the capital arguably should get a larger share of the profits. Do not rely on a form contract you download from the web when it comes to profit-sharing arrangements (or any other issue, for that matter). The allocation of profits among the partners should be tailored to the specifics of the partnership's business or the individual attributes of the partners.

2. *Sharing Losses*

Partners do not need to reach an explicit agreement on how they will share the partnership's losses. Unless otherwise agreed, under UPA § 18(a) and RUPA § 401(b), partners share losses *in the same proportion as they share in the profits*. Again, this arrangement may not be suitable in every case. Naturally, partners can agree to split profits one way and losses in a different manner, but in the absence of such an agreement, *losses follow profits*.

It may surprise you to learn that partners share the partnership's *capital* losses, not just its operating losses. Assume A and B form a partnership. A contributes $100,000 in capital; B contributes the expertise needed to manage the firm. If the business goes belly-up and A's $100,000 capital contribution is lost, B (and you!) may be dumbfounded to learn that B is responsible for half of A's capital loss, or $50,000! Even worse, under UPA § 18(f) and RUPA § 401(h), B is *not* entitled to compensation for his services unless A and B have agreed that B should be paid!

These statutory default rules clearly favor a capital provider over a service provider. One court tried to justify this bias by claiming that a capital provider loses money while the service provider loses nothing. Didn't the court ever hear the expression, "Time is money"? A service provider has opportunity costs, too.

Many people do not want to raise these issues at the outset of a new business venture because they are afraid that flagging potential problems may put the kibosh on the deal. Maybe so, but if they do not contract around the default rules (equal profits, equal losses, liability for capital contributions, no compensation), the default rules will apply to their business. There is an important lesson here: you must know what the statute says to be able to draft around it! That is exactly what B should have done in the example above: get A to agree that B is not liable for any part of A's capital contribution and that B is to be compensated for his managerial services. Getting an agreement: good. Getting it in a signed writing: priceless!

Some courts, including the California Supreme Court, have tried to redress this imbalance by holding that the default rule on capital repayment does not apply where one partner contributes all the capital and the other contributes only services—even though that conclusion contradicts the express language of the statute. *See Kovacik v. Reed*, 40 Cal. 2d 166, 315 P.2d 314 (1957). As expected, the drafters of RUPA explicitly reject the California approach. The Comment to RUPA § 401 reaffirms that the only way to avoid the default rule is to *contract around it*.

Sharing losses is also germane when it comes to a *joint venture*. The term "joint venture" makes it sound like the firm has a narrower scope than a general partnership, but that is not necessarily the case. A joint venture may have a broad scope, while a general partnership may be formed for a limited term or to achieve a particular task. In practice, it does not matter; joint ventures are governed by general partnership law. Whether a business is designated a "joint venture" or a "general partnership," the result will be the same.

There is one wrinkle, however, in forming a joint venture: to form a joint venture, there must be an *explicit* agreement on how the losses will be shared. By contrast, no explicit agreement on sharing losses is needed to form a general partnership since the statutory default rules provide that losses follow profits if the partners have not agreed otherwise. This wrinkle notwithstanding, however, a joint venture is exactly like a general partnership. For simplicity's sake, think **"JV = GP"**!

H. Partnership Dissolution Under the UPA

Dissolution of a partnership under the UPA is the most complex and confusing area of partnership law. Much of the confusion stems from the UPA's aggregate approach to partnerships, which treats partners and their partnership as one and the same. RUPA solves many of the problems created by the UPA by viewing a partnership as an entity distinct from the partners. Moreover, the framework adopted by RUPA for the end of a partnership's life cycle reflects the way things work in the real world today. Let's first take a look at the relevant provisions of the UPA and then explore how RUPA has simplified and streamlined the process.

1. Definition

As we saw previously, a partnership is defined under UPA § 6 as an *association* of two or more persons to carry on as co-owners of a business for profit. In accordance with this definition, under UPA § 29, a partnership is dissolved when a partner ceases to be *associated* in carrying on the partnership's business. Consider for a moment how fragile a partnership is: when a partner leaves, for any reason, the partnership dissolves. This is the second worst aspect of operating as a general partnership (after personal liability): it is so easily dissolved. However, watch out! The term "dissolution" is misleading. A partnership does *not* terminate on dissolution! The UPA § 29 envisions that once a partnership dissolves, partnership affairs will be wound up, and only *then* will the partnership terminate.

The following diagram (not to scale) shows how dissolution and termination fit into the life cycle of a partnership under the UPA:

```
                                 Winding up
|_____|_____|
Formation              Dissolution       Termination
```

2. Causes of Dissolution

Now that you are familiar with what dissolution means, we can examine the causes of dissolution embodied in UPA § 31 and § 32:

— the end of a partnership's term or the accomplishment of a specific undertaking;

— a partner's express will;

— an event that makes it illegal to carry on the partnership's business;

— the expulsion of a partner in accordance with the partnership agreement;

— a partner's death;

— the bankruptcy of a partner or the partnership; and

— the issuance of a court decree.

Most of these causes are pretty straightforward, but a few warrant additional scrutiny.

3. Distinguishing Rightful from Wrongful Dissolution

A "term partnership" is formed to last for a specified period of time (e.g., a partnership with a two-year term) or until a specific task has been accomplished (e.g., a partnership to make a movie). Once the two years are up or the movie has been made, the partnership will automatically dissolve. In other words, a term partnership has a *built-in ending.*

The tricky thing about a term partnership is that a partner has the *power* to dissolve a term partnership by his express will before the term is up. However, if he does, he will be *liable to the other partners for breach of contract.* Think of it this way: a partner in a term partnership is like any other contracting party. If he chooses not to perform his part of the bargain, he is liable for breach of contract. This type of exit by a partner is known as a **wrongful dissolution.** The partner agreed to stick around until the term was up, then changed his mind in violation of the partnership agreement. That is what makes his dissolution "wrongful."

Example #9

Kelly, John, Blake and Gwen form a partnership *to buy land, subdivide it, and sell off the lots.* This is a *term partnership.* The partnership was formed to accomplish a specific task—selling off the lots. Before any of the lots is sold, Kelly lets the others know she wants out. Kelly has *wrongfully dissolved* because she left the partnership before the last lot was sold. As a result, she will be liable to her partners for breach of contract.

Unlike a term partnership, a **"partnership at will"** does not have a built-in ending. An at-will partnership is open-ended; theoretically, it can go on forever. In the real world, most partnerships are at will—*i.e.,* they exist at the will of the partners. A partner in an at-will partnership may dissolve the partnership by his express will *at any time* without liability to the other partners for breach. Why can he do this? Because he never agreed to stick around for a specified time or until a particular result was achieved. His dissolution is *rightful.*

Example #10

Kelly, John, Blake and Gwen form a partnership *to give voice lessons.* This is a *partnership at will*—no built-in ending. After a week, Kelly lets the others know she wants out. Kelly has *not* wrongfully dissolved the partnership. She was free to leave any time she liked. Kelly is not liable to her partners for breach of contract.

It is sometimes said that a partner in a partnership at will has the *right* to dissolve, whereas a partner in a term partnership has only the *power* to dissolve (he can dissolve if he wants to, but he will be liable for breach of contract). This "right" versus "power" distinction is often used as a shorthand to differentiate a *rightful* dissolution from a *wrongful* one.

4. *Dissolution at a Court's Discretion*

Alternatively, a party who has no right to dissolve may ask the court to dissolve the partnership. UPA § 32 provides that a court "shall" decree dissolution (1) where a partner has been guilty of conduct prejudicial to partnership's business or persistently breached the partnership agreement; (2) when the partnership's business can only be carried on at a loss; (3) if other circumstances render a dissolution equitable; or (4) in certain other limited situations. Be apprised, however, that courts have uniformly construed the word "shall" to mean "may." Regardless of the facts, a court is never obligated to dissolve a partnership.

If a court declines to dissolve the partnership, the partner seeking dissolution is stuck. He can try to sell his interest in the partnership, but who would buy it? He is unlikely to find a buyer willing to step into his shoes. His only option (other than wrongful dissolution) would be to try renegotiating a buyout with the other partner(s), or perhaps see a marriage counselor with them. After all, as Cardozo said in *Meinhard v. Salmon*, partners are in it "for better or worse"!

5.   *Effects of Rightful and Wrongful Dissolution*

Under the UPA, things are much better for a partner who rightfully dissolves a partnership. That partner has a choice: he can either (a) require that partnership affairs be wound up and force liquidation pursuant to UPA § 38(1), or (b) have the partnership buy him out and let the partnership's business continue without him under UPA § 42.

The first option is draconian. If the partnership's business cannot be sold as an ongoing concern, the firm's assets are liquidated, its liabilities paid off, and partners are paid their capital contributions and profit shares *in cash*. Where assets are sold off piece by piece, the value of the firm's "goodwill" (reputation) is lost. Fortunately, partners are permitted to contract around this option.

Pursuant to the second option, Section 42 allows the dissolving partner to let the partnership's business continue, while the partnership itself is dissolved. In other words, the non-departing partners may continue the partnership's business, but under a new partnership—one without the departing partner. In exchange, the departing partner is bought out and receives the value of his interest in the partnership as of the date of dissolution plus either a market rate of interest or, at the departing partner's option, his share of profits from dissolution until termination. Partners may vary the terms of the buyout if they so desire in their partnership agreement.

In contrast, UPA § 38(2) provides that a partner who *wrongfully* dissolves a partnership cannot force liquidation. His only option is a buyout, less whatever damages he owes for breach of contract. Moreover, a wrongfully dissolving partner is not compensated for the value of the firm's good-will. Thus, a partner who wrongfully dissolves is considerably worse off than a partner who is within his rights to dissolve the partnership.

6. *Winding up Partnership Affairs*

Winding up, sometimes referred to as "liquidation," involves the process of selling off the partnership's assets, paying off the partnership's creditors, and distributing profits or losses among the partners.

Under UPA § 37, any partner who has not wrongfully dissolved the partnership is entitled to wind up partnership affairs, unless the partners have agreed otherwise. The partner who winds up the business *is* entitled to compensation from the partnership for performing this task, unlike a partner who renders other services to the partnership. See UPA § 18(f). The partnership is responsible for any expenses incurred during the winding up process.

Part of the winding up process involves applying the partnership's assets to pay off its liabilities. Section 40 of the UPA provides the following hierarchy for the paying off partnership obligations:

— Third-party creditors are paid off first.

— Then partners who are creditors are repaid.

— Next, partners get back their capital contributions.

— Finally, if there is anything left, the balance is paid to the partners according to their profit shares per UPA § 18.

The mechanics are discomforting for the mathematically challenged, so let's break down Section 40 step-by-step in the context of a hypothetical fact pattern.

ABC Partnership ("ABC") has $100,000 in assets. ABC owes $30,000 to a third-party creditor and $15,000 to B for a loan. A and

B each contributed $5,000 capital. C contributed only services. If ABC dissolves, what happens in winding up ABC?

First, ABC pays the third-party creditor $30,000 (leaving $70,000). Next, ABC pays B $15,000 in repayment of the loan (leaving $55,000). ABC then repays A and B for their $5,000 capital contributions (leaving $45,000). Lastly, ABC distributes the $45,000 balance to A, B and C equally, unless they agreed to split profits another way. The math looks like this:

> $100,000 in partnership assets
> – $ 30,000 to the third-party creditor
> – $ 15,000 to B for the loan
> – $ 10,000 return of capital to A and B
> $ 45,000 profit split equally ($15,000 each)

If the partnership's assets are insufficient to cover the partnership's liabilities, apply the same payment hierarchy until the partnership runs out of assets. At that point, the partners must shoulder the remaining liabilities in the same proportion in which they share profits, unless otherwise agreed.

Let's see how this arrangement plays out in a variation on our hypo. Assume ABC has the same liabilities, but only $35,000 in assets. ABC first pays the third-party creditor $30,000, then pays B the $5,000 that is left. The remaining $10,000 due B on the loan and A's and B's $5,000 capital contributions are partnership losses, which A, B and C must bear equally under the default rule, unless they agreed to share losses differently. Here is the math:

$35,000 in partnership assets

− $30,000 to third-party creditor

− $ 5,000 to B for the loan

$ 0

($10,000) remaining balance owed to B on the loan

($10,000) capital contributions from A and B

($20,000) loss split equally ($6,667 each)

You may be wondering: how do we equalize the losses among the partners? Work it through. A is already $5,000 in the hole from losing his capital contribution, so if A contributes $1,667 to B, A would be out a total of $6,667. C gives B his $6,667 share of the loss. B ends up with $8,334 of the $15,000 the partnership owes him for the loan and his capital, leaving B with a deficit of $6,666. Viola! Each partner is left bearing one-third of the loss. Of course, if A and C have no assets, B is out of luck.

You may wonder why C did not receive compensation for the services he contributed to the partnership when we were dividing up the partnership's assets. Recall that the default rules in UPA § 18 favor capital providers over service providers: no compensation for services rendered to the partnership in the absence of an agreement. Therefore, C's services go uncompensated, unless A, B, and C had previously agreed that C should be compensated for the services.

One final note on winding up. Don't sweat it if you cannot do the math or are afraid to try (believe me, you are not alone). You will get the lion's share of the credit on your BA final or on the bar exam if you simply recite the repayment hierarchy under the UPA § 40. That way, your professor or the bar examiners can see that you know the applicable rule. Leave the number-crunching to a CPA (as you will when you are a practicing attorney).

7. Post-Dissolution Liability

We know that a partnership is liable for any expenses incurred in winding up. That is just common sense. However, the partnership may also be liable on post-dissolution contracts having nothing to do with winding up! That may seem counterintuitive. How can the partnership be liable for *new* business when the partnership has been dissolved?

Liability is based on our old friend *apparent authority*. We hold the partnership liable to protect an *innocent* third party. Even though the partnership has been dissolved, a third party may not be aware of the dissolution. In that case, we hold the partnership liable to a third party on a post-dissolution contract where a partner *appeared* to have authority to bind the partnership to the third party.

However, Section 35 of the UPA lets the partnership protect itself against liability for new business after dissolution by notifying potential creditors that the partnership has been dissolved. *Prior creditors* of the partnership are entitled to *personal* notice because the partnership has their names and addresses. By contrast, a person who *knew* of the partnership before dissolution, but was not a prior creditor, is entitled to *newspaper* notice. The partnership does not have such a person's contact information, so the best the partnership can do is put a notice in the local newspaper advertising its dissolution. Finally, people who did not even know about the partnership before dissolution cannot hold the partnership liable for new business after dissolution, and thus they are not entitled to any notice at all.

Example #11

Kelly dissolves the partnership. Target had sold goods on credit to the partnership before dissolution. Acting with apparent authority to bind the partnership, Gwen contracts with Target again after dissolution. Target did not know the partnership had dissolved and had not received personal notice of dissolution. The partnership will be liable to Target on the post-dissolution obligation. Please note that when it comes to the partnership's liability *to a third party* on a post-dissolution obligation, the *cause* of dissolution is *irrelevant*.

Example #12

Same facts as Example #11, except that the partnership advertised its dissolution in the local newspaper. The partnership will still be liable to Target on the post-dissolution obligation. As a prior creditor, Target was entitled to receive *personal notice* of the dissolution. Therefore, newspaper notice is not sufficient to protect the partnership against liability to Target on the post-dissolution contract. This trick question is a bar examiner favorite!

It may be obvious, but it is worth noting that people who *know* about a partnership's dissolution have no rights against the partnership for new business after dissolution, even if the partnership failed to provide them with proper notice. Those foolish folks assumed the risk of non-payment by the dissolved firm.

If the partnership is liable on a post-dissolution obligation, the partners are liable on the obligation, too. A partner's liability is the same regardless of when a partnership obligation arises. As we saw earlier, under the UPA § 15, partners are jointly liable for contracts, and joint and several liability for torts. However, there is a narrow exception in UPA § 35(2) for a **"silent partner."** A partner is not liable for new business after dissolution when the partner was *unknown* as a partner to the person with whom the contract was made and was *so inactive* in partnership affairs that the reputation of the partnership could not be said to have been due to his connection with it. As you can imagine, this "silent partner" exception does not apply very often.

Whether a partner can get contribution from the other partners on a post-dissolution obligation depends on two things: (1) the *cause* of dissolution and (2) whether the partner acting for the partnership was *aware* that the partnership had been dissolved.

Under UPA § 34, contribution *is* available if dissolution was caused by the death or bankruptcy of a partner *and* the partner acting for the partnership did not *know or have notice* of the death or bankruptcy. When dissolution is caused by a partner's act (*e.g.*, a partner's express will), contribution is available *only* if the partner acting for the partnership did not *know* about the dissolution. Contribution is not available at all if the partnership was dissolved in any other way. Presumably, a partner ought to know, for example, when the partnership's term is up, or that a court has ordered the partnership to dissolve, so he should not have entered a new contract for the dissolved partnership at all.

Example #13

Same facts as in Example #11 and Example #12. The partnership is liable to Target on the post-dissolution obligation. If Gwen pays Target off, Gwen's right to get contribution from the other partners will depend on the *cause* of dissolution. For example, if Kelly dissolved by her *express will*, Gwen can get contribution if she did not *know* of the dissolution when she contracted with Target. By contrast, if the partnership was dissolved by Kelly's *death*, Gwen can get contribution only if she did not *know or have notice* of Kelly's death when she contracted with Target. When it comes to a partner's *right to get contribution* on a post-dissolution obligation, the *cause* of dissolution is *relevant*.

8. Effect of Dissolution on Partner's Existing Liability

Section 36 of the UPA makes clear that dissolution does not discharge a partner's liability for pre-existing obligations. Thus, a partner cannot avoid existing liability merely by leaving the firm.

In the event the partnership's business continues after dissolution, existing creditors of the dissolved partnership automatically become creditors of the persons continuing the business. However, a creditor and the partners who continue the business may agree to *release* the dissolving partner from an existing obligation. *Please note*: a partner cannot be released by a creditor *alone*. Those who are continuing the partnership's business must consent to the release because they will be picking up the slack for the partner who is relieved of his liability.

The release need not be expressly granted. A release is *inferred* where a creditor with knowledge of the dissolution continues to do business with the firm. *See* UPA § 36(2). In that instance, the creditor has assumed the risk of doing business with the new partnership and the continuing partners and can no longer rely on the assets of the departing partner.

9. Jingle Rule

The UPA § 40 also addresses the relative rights of partnership creditors and an individual partner's separate creditors regarding distributions made during the winding up process. Partnership creditors have priority on partnership property, while separate creditors have priority on separate property. This is colorfully referred to as the "jingle rule" because someone thought it sounded like an advertising jingle (partnership/partnership, separate/separate). Whether you think so or not, you are stuck with the term.

I.   Dissociation and Winding up Under RUPA

1.   Overview

RUPA has a very different take on the end of a partnership's life cycle, so different that RUPA's approach merits a section of its own. This area marks RUPA's greatest divergence from the UPA. RUPA uses different terminology and adopts a completely different analytical framework. More important for your purposes: it is a lot easier to grasp than the corresponding provisions of the UPA.

Although RUPA § 202(a) defines a partnership an association of two or more persons, RUPA § 201(a) explicitly acknowledges that a partnership is an *entity* distinct from the partners. For that reason, a partner's leaving the partnership *does not* cause the partnership to dissolve. The partnership as an entity continues to exist without the departing partner.

RUPA uses the term "dissociation" to refer to a partner's departure from the partnership. The term is a clever play on words: "dissociation" is the opposite of "association." In essence, it is a *dis-association*. The main thing to remember is this: *a partner's dissociation is usually no big deal!*

Only certain specified events require winding up and dissolution (see below). If winding up is not required, and it rarely is, the partnership must buy out the dissociating partner for the fair market value of his interest in the partnership unless the partnership agreement provides otherwise. Thus, under RUPA, the partnership simply pays the dissociating partner off and continues in business without him! However, a partner who dissociates from a term partnership prematurely will be liable to the other partners for damages for his "wrongful" dissociation.

This approach is more in keeping with how things work in practice: a partner leaves, but the partnership lives on. Imagine that you form a law firm partnership with friends after graduating from law school and passing the bar. After six months, you decide you would rather practice solo. What will likely happen when you leave? Your partners will buy you out, wave goodbye, and continue in business without you. Adios, amigo.

2. *Consequences of Dissociation*

Still, dissociation has consequences for both the dissociating partner and the partnership. First, dissociation does not discharge a dissociating partner's liability for pre-existing obligations, unless he is released from liability for a particular obligation. In this regard, RUPA is like the UPA.

Second, under RUPA § 702, for two years after dissociation, the dissociating partner continues to have *apparent authority* to bind the partnership to a third party who reasonably believes the dissociated partner is still a partner and who does not have notice or constructive knowledge of the dissociation. There are two ways a partnership can shield itself against such liability. It can either (a) *notify* creditors of the dissociation (effective immediately) or (b) it can submit for filing a *Statement of Dissociation* to the Secretary of State (becomes effective 90 days after it is filed). Once effective, the Statement of Dissociation provides creditors with *constructive knowledge* that the dissociated partner no longer has authority to bind the partnership. If it turns out the partnership is liable on the post-dissociation obligation, the dissociating partner must reimburse the partnership for any resulting damage.

Lastly, a dissociating partner can still be held liable to an innocent third party for partnership obligations incurred within two years after dissociation. To protect against this liability, a dissociating partner may notify potential partnership creditors (effective immediately) or submit a Statement of Dissociation (becomes effective 90 days after it is filed by the Secretary of

State). Here, what is good for the goose (the partnership) is good for the gander (the dissociating partner). Either one can file a Statement of Dissociation for self-protection.

3. *Events Requiring Dissolution*

Under RUPA, "dissolution" is simply the beginning of the winding up process. As mentioned above, only certain events require dissolution and the winding up of partnership affairs under RUPA. Those events are:

— an event specified in the partnership agreement that requires winding up;

— an event that makes it unlawful for the partnership's business to continue;

— a judicial determination requiring dissolution;

— in a partnership at will, a partner's express will to withdraw; and

— in a term partnership, either

a.   the expiration of the term or the completion of the undertaking,

b.   the express will of all partners to wind up, or

c.   within 90 days after a partner's death or wrongful dissociation, the express will of at least half the remaining partners to wind up.

If an event requiring dissolution and winding up does occur, all the partners, including the dissociating partner, may waive their right to have the partnership's business wound up and the partnership terminated. *See* RUPA § 802. In that event, the partnership resumes business as if it had never been dissolved. Again, no big deal! For the record, the consent of a wrongfully dissociating partner (a partner who dissociated in violation of the partnership agreement) is not required to continue the business.

Partners who have not wrongfully dissociated may wind up partnership affairs. The partnership is liable for any expenses incurred in winding up.

4. Post-Dissolution Liability

As under the UPA, a RUPA partnership is liable for new business after dissolution based on a partner's apparent authority if the other party to the transaction did not have notice of the dissolution. However, the cumbersome notice requirements of the UPA that prescribe different kinds of notice for different kinds of creditors are eliminated in RUPA in favor of apparent authority.

To protect the partnership against potential liability on *new* business after dissolution, any partner who did not wrongfully dissociate may submit a *Statement of Dissolution* to the Secretary of State for filing. Like a Statement of Dissociation, a Statement of Dissolution becomes effective 90 days after it is filed by the Secretary of State. Once effective, the Statement of Dissolution provides creditors with *constructive notice* that the partners' authority is limited to transactions appropriate for winding up partnership affairs.

If a partnership is liable for new business after dissolution, the partner who incurred the liability must reimburse the partnership for any resulting damage if he *knew* of the dissolution when he incurred the obligation. He knew he should not do it, but he did it anyway. Ante up!

5. Winding up

If a partnership expense is incurred in winding up or in new business, all the partners are liable for the expense. Recall that under RUPA § 306, partners are jointly and severally liable for *all* partnership obligations *no matter when they arise.* FYI, there is no post-dissolution exception for a "silent partner" under RUPA as there is under the UPA.

In winding up a partnership's business, the partnership's assets are applied to pay off its liabilities. RUPA's default rules in Section 807 are like the UPA's default rules, but there are two major differences. First, under RUPA, third-party creditors do not get priority over partners who are creditors; instead, all creditors are treated *on a par* with one another. Second, RUPA abolishes the UPA "jingle rule." Partnership creditors still get priority on the distribution of partnership property, but separate creditors no longer get priority on the distribution of separate property.

6. *Prepare for the End Game*

Under both the UPA and RUPA, partners can contract around the statutory default rules by spelling out in their partnership agreement what will happen in the endgame. The agreement should cover key issues. For example, who will finance the buyout—the partnership, the partners, or some combination of the two? How much will the departing partner receive? If a sum will be paid out over time, for how long and at what interest rate? What events trigger the payout? It is important to tailor the compensation scheme to the partnership's business. Careful drafting is crucial. Courts will generally enforce these agreements if they are the result of an arm's length bargain, even where the sum the partner is to receive is well below the market value of his stake in the partnership.

Partners may also want to consider adding a *non-competition clause* to protect against competition from a partner who leaves the partnership. The scope and duration of a non-competition clause must be *reasonable* in terms of scope and duration. Courts tend to construe "non-competes" narrowly because they have the potential to operate as a restraint on alienation (*i.e.*, they may prevent someone from earning a living in his chosen field). If a court determines that the clause is deficient in one or more respects, the court may narrow the clause to make it reasonable or strike it down altogether, depending on the court's approach to overly broad non-competition clauses.

Example #14

John, Paul, George and Ringo form a partnership. Their partnership agreement provides that if any partner leaves the partnership, he may not compete with the partnership anywhere in the U.S. for ten years. If a court finds this clause to be unreasonably broad, it may narrow the clause to impose reasonable limits (*e.g.*, no competition for two years in Texas) or it may strike the clause in its entirety, depending on the jurisdiction.

Furthermore, a non-competition clause may be prohibited by state law in certain circumstances. For example, the New York Court of Appeals held that a non-competition clause in a law firm partnership agreement was unenforceable because of the potential harm to clients of the departing partner. Non-competes for other partnerships, however, are allowed. I guess lawyers have a strong lobby in New York.

J.   Conversion and Merger

The UPA is silent about converting or merging a general partnership into a different business form. That is not surprising. When the UPA was promulgated in 1914, neither conversion nor merger of a general partnership was an issue. With the proliferation of many new types of business associations in the late twentieth century, switching from one form of business to another became more commonplace. RUPA (1997) permits a general partnership to convert into a limited partnership (and vice versa). RUPA (2013) goes further, allowing a general partnership to convert into *any* other type of business association, not just into a limited partnership.

1. *Conversion*

Under RUPA (1997), a general partnership may *convert* into a limited partnership by following a two-step process. First, the terms of the conversion must be approved by *all* the partners, or by the number or percentage of partners specified for conversion in the partnership agreement. Second, the partnership must submit a Certificate of Limited Partnership to the Secretary of State. The conversion takes effect when the Certificate of Limited Partnership is filed by the Secretary of State.

Conversion does not change a partner's liability for *existing* obligations. He remains liable for any obligation incurred by the general partnership before the conversion took effect. [The issue of when a debt is "incurred" is discussed below under Limited Liability Partnerships.]

Conversion of a limited partnership into a general partnership requires the approval of *all* the partners, *even if the limited partnership agreement provides otherwise*. The conversion takes effect when the Certificate of Limited Partnership is *cancelled*. Former limited partners remain shielded from liability for obligations incurred *before* conversion, but they are liable as general partners for obligations incurred *after* conversion.

To avoid any confusion, RUPA (2013) § 1146 makes it clear that a general partnership or a limited partnership that has been converted is for all purposes the same entity that existed before the conversion.

2. *Merger*

A general partnership may be merged with one or more general partnerships or limited partnerships. A plan of merger must be approved by all the partners, or by a number or percentage specified for a merger in the partnership agreement. The merger generally takes effect once the plan has been approved by all parties to the merger.

After a merger takes effect, the separate existence of each party to the merger ceases. All property owned by each of the constituent firms vests in the surviving entity, and their obligations become obligations of the surviving entity.

Under RUPA (1997), the surviving entity *may* submit a Statement of Merger to the Secretary of State for filing. Under RUPA (2013), however, a Statement of Merger *must* be delivered to the Secretary of State for filing.

CHAPTER 5

Limited Liability Partnerships

A. Overview

One way to maintain the flexibility of a general partnership while avoiding the partners' vicarious liability for partnership obligations is to form a **limited liability partnership** ("**LLP**"). An LLP is like a two-for-the-price-of-one special: you get all the benefits of a general partnership (*e.g.*, flexible management structure and pass-through federal income tax treatment) without *any* risk of personal liability. What's not to like about an LLP? Nothing! It was a *rhetorical* question.

There is no special LLP statute. In fact, LLPs are governed by general partnership law. However, an LLP and a general partnership are not identical. There is one major difference: *partners in an LLP are not personally liable for the firm's obligations*. Admittedly, that is a huge distinction. Nonetheless, it is useful to remember that in almost every other respect, an LLP is treated exactly like a general partnership. For simplicity's sake, think of an LLP as a general partnership minus personal liability: *LLP = GP – personal liability*.

111

B. History of the LLP

A short history lesson is in order about the LLP. The first LLP statute was enacted in Texas in 1991 in response to the savings and loan crisis of the mid-1980s. Creditors of failed savings and loan institutions sought a "deep pocket" from which to recover their losses. The obvious targets were partners in the law firm general partnerships that represented the institutions. As we saw above, *all* the partners at the firm would be personally liable if *any* partner at the firm (or any associate, for that matter) committed malpractice. Yikes! In the aftermath, lawyers lobbied the Texas legislature to pass a bill insulating partners from vicarious liability for torts committed by other people at the firm, unless the tortfeasor was under a partner's *direct control*. The result was the first limited liability partnership statute in the United States. Other states soon followed Texas' lead.

Only four years later, Texas broadened the protection afforded by LLPs to shield partners in an LLP from liability for contract obligations as well as torts committed by other persons. Most states have followed suit, although a few still insulate partners in an LLP only from vicarious *tort* liability (these are known as "*narrow shield*" statutes). Imposing vicarious liability for the torts of persons under a partner's control has also been eliminated in most states.

The increasingly *broad shield* provided by LLP statutes has made the LLP a popular form of business association over the last twenty years. Be apprised, however, that in some states, an LLP is not available to everyone. For example, in New York and California, only those providing professional services, like lawyers and accountants, may form an LLP.

The shift from general partnerships to LLPs has transferred much of the risk of doing business from partners to the third parties who do business with the partnership. With a general partnership, the onus is on *the partners* to get third parties to agree that the partners will not be personally liable on partnership obligations. Conversely, with an LLP, the burden is on *third parties* to get the partners to agree to assume personal liability for the firm's obligations. This seismic shift makes creditors bear the risk of non-payment simply because they have done business with the "wrong" kind of partnership!

One final historical observation: the LLP form of business association was not created until long after the UPA was published. Thus, if you look for LLP provisions in the UPA, you will not find any. Only RUPA addresses LLPs.

C. Forming an LLP

Formation is another area in which an LLP differs from a general partnership. All state statutes require an LLP to include in its name words or initials that identify the firm as an LLP. This requirement is designed to put third parties on notice that the owners of the firm have limited personal liability for the firm's obligations. Still, many people dealing with an LLP do not realize they need to protect themselves in advance, so the liability shield provided by the LLP statute may catch them unaware.

From a policy point of view, is it fair to impose this kind of risk on unsophisticated parties who may not appreciate the risk they are taking? Think back a few months, before you took Business Associations: were you aware of the risk involved in doing business with an LLP (or any other business form that confers limited liability on its owners)? In this arena, a little knowledge is anything but a dangerous thing!

D. Limited Liability for Whom? For What?

It is worth reiterating that an LLP shields the partners from *vicarious* liability. A partner in an LLP remains liable for his *own* torts or malpractice. A tortfeasor cannot avoid liability no matter what form he chooses for his business. Moreover, the LLP itself is liable under agency principles for any LLP obligation that arises. LLP statutes target *vicarious* liability of the *partners*, not the liability of the tortfeasor or the liability of the firm itself.

Limited liability for the partners, however, comes at a price. To form an LLP, one must submit a document (often called a "Certificate of Organization") to the Secretary of State for filing and pay a fee, usually calculated on a "per partner" basis. In addition, some states require an LLP to maintain at least a minimum amount of liability insurance, or to segregate at least the same amount of money in a separate account. Most states, however, decline to impose a minimum insurance requirement on the theory that other business forms offering limited liability need not carry any insurance, so an LLP should not have to either.

An LLP may also be required to renew its status annually and pay additional fees. If an LLP does not renew its status, the partners may lose their liability shield. In the long run, however, the costs associated with operating an LLP are a small price to pay for limiting the personal liability of the partners. Do not be penny wise and pound foolish, as they say—form an LLP, *not* a general partnership.

E. Miscellaneous Aspects of an LLP

Choosing to operate as an LLP may impact the way partners behave. For example, it is possible that partners in an LLP may not be as meticulous as partners in a general partnership since their personal assets are not at risk, but, as yet there is no empirical evidence to support that assertion.

The specific provisions of a particular state LLP statute may have an impact, too. For example, if a statute includes a provision that retains a partner's personal liability for the torts of people under his control, there may be less incentive to supervise other persons who are working at the firm.

F. Transforming a General Partnership into an LLP

A firm operating as a general partnership may opt to become an LLP by following statutory procedure. RUPA § 1001(b) generally requires that the terms on which a general partnership becomes an LLP must be approved by the vote necessary to amend the partnership agreement. This means that becoming an LLP is the equivalent of amending the partnership agreement.

Unless the partners have agreed otherwise, the default rule under RUPA (as well as the UPA) requires a majority of partners to consent to amending a partnership agreement. After the requisite approval, a partnership becomes an LLP by submitting a *Statement of Qualification* to the Secretary of State for filing.

Curiously, a general partnership that becomes an LLP need not notify its clients of the transformation, even though the clients' rights may be affected by the change in form. For the record: becoming an LLP *is not* a conversion or merger under RUPA, so the provisions of the statute that deal with conversion and merger do not apply in the event a general partnership becomes an LLP.

If a general partnership becomes a limited liability partnership, a question may arise about a liability that was incurred *before* the firm became an LLP. The answer seems relatively straight-forward: if an obligation was incurred while the firm was a general partnership, the partners are personally liable for it. If an obligation was incurred *after* the general partnership became an LLP, the partners are not personally liable for the obligation.

The problem is: how do you determine *when* the obligation was *incurred*? For example, a general partnership executes a five-year lease. One year later, it becomes an LLP. Are the partners liable for rent that *subsequently* comes due? The answer depends on whether the obligation to pay rent was "incurred": when the lease was *signed* or when the rent became *due*?

While resolution of this question is left to principles of contract law, the Comment to RUPA § 306 takes the position that "partnership obligations under or relating to a note, contract, or other agreement generally are incurred *when the note, contract, or other agreement is made*" rather than when the obligation becomes due (emphasis added). As a consequence, the partners would be personally liable because the obligation was incurred by a general partnership. Nonetheless, courts have reached inconsistent results. Third parties may cite the Comment to RUPA § 306 in an attempt to hold the partners liable for the rental payment, but a court is not bound by the comments to RUPA. Despite the Comment, there is no assurance third parties will prevail in their quest to recover from the partners on the remaining lease payments.

With respect to tort liability, the Comment provides that "[p]artnership obligations under or relating to a tort are incurred *when the tort conduct occurs* rather than at the time of the actual injury or harm" (emphasis added). Obviously, a court is not bound by this aspect of the Comment either.

G. Losing LLP Status

To maintain its status as an LLP under RUPA § 1003, an LLP must file an annual report, accompanied by a filing fee. If an LLP fails to file the report and/or pay the fee, the Secretary of State may revoke the firm's LLP status, exposing the partners to personal liability for firm obligations arising *after* the revocation.

Regardless, an LLP whose status has been revoked may apply for reinstatement within two years after revocation. If the application is granted, the reinstatement is *retroactive* to the date of revocation, thereby preventing a gap in the partners' liability shield. What a relief!

PART III

Limited Partnerships

CHAPTER 6

Overview of Limited Partnerships

A limited partnership is a partnership with two types of partners: *general partners,* who are personally liable for the firm's obligations, and *limited partners* who have limited liability. In terms of personal liability, a limited partnership is *better* than a general partnership, because at least *some* partners have limited liability. On the other hand, a limited partnership is *not* as good as a limited liability partnership, where *all the partners* are shielded from vicarious liability. Do not confuse a limited partnership with a limited liability partnership; the names are confusingly similar, but the liability of the partners is very different!

A. Liability of Limited Partners

1. The Uniform Limited Partnership Act (1916)

The most notable development in limited partnership law over the last century has been the expansion of protection for limited partners at the expense of a limited partnership's creditors. The Uniform Limited Partnership Act ("ULPA"), adopted by the National Council of Commissioners on Uniform State Law ("NCCUSL") in 1916, conferred limited liability on a limited partner "unless he takes part in the *control* of the business." ULPA § 7 (emphasis added). A limited partner who participated in control was liable to the same extent as a general partner. Basically, a limited partner got limited liability in exchange for giving up the right to control the limited partnership's business.

Unfortunately, ULPA did not define "control," so there was no hard-and-fast rule to determine whether a limited partner had exercised "control." As a result, although ULPA was adopted in every state except Louisiana, courts reached inconsistent results about the scope of the control rule. For example, some courts found that a limited partner who was also a director of a corporate general partner had participated in control, while other courts reached the opposite conclusion. Courts also disagreed about other issues, like whether a limited partner who had veto power over business decisions had taken part in control.

The uncertainty generated by these conflicting decisions cast doubt on the efficacy of operating as a limited partnership. If potential investors, *i.e.*, potential limited partners, had doubts about whether they would be shielded from personal liability if they invested and became limited partners, they were less likely to invest in a limited partnership. They would just as soon invest in a different kind of business association that assured them that their personal assets would not be available to pay off the firm's obligations.

2. *The Revised Uniform Limited Partnership Act (1976)*

In 1976, NCCUSL adopted a revised version of ULPA. Revision was long overdue because limited partnerships had changed significantly in the intervening sixty years. In 1916, most limited partnerships operated locally with just a few partners. By 1976, limited partnerships attracted hundreds of investors from across the country who sought to take advantage of tax-sheltered limited partnerships. In a tax shelter, investors use paper losses generated by the limited partnership, like depreciation and depletion, to offset ("shelter") income from other sources,[1] thereby reducing their taxable income. Score: limited partners 1, IRS 0.

In terms of liability, RULPA (1976) benefits limited partners in two significant respects. First, although RULPA (1976) § 303 does not define what constitutes "control," it does include a *non-exclusive* list of things a limited partner can do without exercising control. These "safe harbors" are generous. They allow limited partners to engage in a variety of activities without running afoul of the control test, including (1) being a contractor for or an agent or employee of the limited partnership or a general partner; (2) consulting with and advising a general partner on the business of the limited partnership; and (3) acting as a surety for the limited partnership. The safe harbors eliminate much of the uncertainty that plagued courts under ULPA.

More significantly, RULPA (1976) reduces the ambit of liability for a limited partner who exercises control. RULPA (1976) adopts a two-pronged control test. Under the first prong, if a limited partner's participation in control is substantially the same as a general partner's, he is liable like a general partner to *all* the limited partnership's creditors. Nothing newsworthy there. It is the second prong that breaks new ground: if a limited partner's participation in control is *not* substantially the same as a general partner's, "he is liable *only* to persons who transact business with the limited partnership with *actual knowledge* of his participation

---

[1]   A "paper loss" is a loss reflected on a balance sheet that is not an out-of-pocket loss for investors. Depreciation is one example. Certain assets, like a building, wear out over time and must eventually be replaced. Depreciation allocates a portion of that wear and tear to each year the asset is used. This results in a tax deduction. The building, however, may be *increasing* in value! That is what makes the depreciation deduction a "paper loss."

in control." RULPA (1976) § 303 (emphasis added). Under this second prong, only partnership creditors who have *actual contact* with a limited partner can hold him liable for a partnership obligation. Consequently, there is much less risk that a limited partner will be held personally liable to the firm's creditors under RULPA (1976) than under ULPA. Not surprisingly, RULPA (1976) was widely adopted.

3. *The Revised Uniform Limited Partnership Act (1985)*

Only nine years later, RULPA was revised again to further reduce a limited partner's liability for participating in control. First, RULPA (1985) § 303 expanded the list of safe harbors. Second, it eliminated blanket liability for a limited partner who participated in control by adopting a *reliance test*: a limited partner who participates in control is liable *only* to a third party who is *misled by the limited partner's conduct* into believing that the limited partner is a general partner. This test is applied on a creditor-by-creditor basis. As a result, the liability of limited partners to third parties under the control rule became even more remote.

We know that general partners are liable for a limited partnership's obligations. But what if the only general partner is a minimally-capitalized corporation that is run by limited partners? The limited partners can argue that they did not participate in control of the limited partnership because they were acting in their *corporate* capacity, on behalf of the corporate general partner. Some courts saw this argument as brazen attempt to make an "end run" around the control test. They found limited partners liable for exercising control over the limited partnership's business in this scenario by disregarding the existence of the corporation.

RULPA (1985) § 303(b)(1) effectively overturned these decisions by establishing a safe harbor for being an officer, director, or shareholder of a corporate general partner. The bottom line is that if you deal with a limited partnership that has a corporation as its only general partner, you need to protect yourself in advance or you will not be able to recover from the limited partners under RULPA (1985).

4. The Uniform Limited Partnership Act (2001)

In 2001, NCCUSL finally took the plunge and eliminated the control rule altogether. Thus, in states that have adopted ULPA (2001),[2] creditors of a limited partnership cannot hold limited partners personally liable for the firm's obligations even if they take part in control! As we saw with LLPs, the onus of protecting oneself has shifted from the partners to third-party creditors. (The latest revision in 2013 also eliminates the control rule.)

5. Comparative Timelines

The following chart compares the test for determining if a limited partner is liable for exercising control as well as the extent of his liability under each version of ULPA/RULPA noted above:

---

[2] ULPA (2001) is much longer and more complex than earlier versions of RULPA. Because it is intended to "stand alone," the drafters designated it the "Uniform Limited Partnership Art" rather than a "Revised" version of ULPA.

Comparison of the Control Test and the Liability of Limited Partners Over Time Under ULPA/RULPA

Version	Test	Liability for control
1916	Control (no guidance)	Same as a **general partner**
1976	Control (safe harbors)	
	If substantially like a general partner	Same as a **general partner**
	If not substantially like a general partner	Only to third party with *actual knowledge of control*
1985	Control (*expanded* safe harbors)	Only to third party *misled by a limited partner's conduct*
2001/2013	No control test	*No liability for control*

The following diagram offers a different perspective on the same trend. Narrowing/eliminating the control test has made it more difficult, if not impossible, for third-party creditors of a limited partnership to recover from limited partners. This diagram graphically illustrates the *diminishing protection of third parties* under successive versions of ULPA/RULPA (it resembles an upside-down pyramid):

Protection of Creditors in a Limited Partnership Over Time

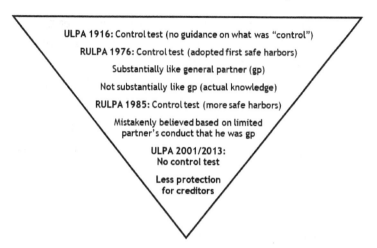

ULPA 1916: Control test (no guidance on what was "control")

RULPA 1976: Control test (adopted first safe harbors)

Substantially like general partner (gp)

Not substantially like gp (actual knowledge)

RULPA 1985: Control test (more safe harbors)

Mistakenly believed based on limited partner's conduct that he was gp

ULPA 2001/2013: No control test

Less protection for creditors

BOTTOM LINE: The changes in the Uniform Limited Partnership Act beginning in 1976 increasingly protect the limited partners *at the expense of creditors* who deal with a limited partnership.

B. Linkage with the General Partnership Statute

Traditionally, if the limited partnership statute was silent on a given issue, courts looked to the general partnership statute to fill the gap. In that sense, the limited partnership and general partnership statutes were *linked*. However, ULPA (2001) and ULPA (2013) are designed to be *stand-alone statutes* unlinked from general partnership law. Under those statutes, what will a court do if it finds a gap? It will most likely look to general partnership law anyway. In any event, because ULPA (2001) and ULPA (2013) have not been widely adopted, linkage is still an important concept in most states.

C. Formation of a Limited Partnership

Certain formalities are required to form a limited partnership. Because RULPA (1985) has been adopted in most states, it will serve as our paradigm, but the specific formalities required vary from state to state, so be sure to check the applicable statute for relevant details.

As with other business associations that limit liability, the organizer must submit a document (called a "Certificate of Limited Partnership") to the Secretary of State for filing, along with a fee. The Certificate must be signed by all the *general* partners.

By design, the Certificate is not very informative. Instead, the authoritative and comprehensive document for most limited partnerships is the partnership agreement (see below), not the Certificate of Limited Partnership. In fact, the *only* information that must be included in the Certificate is the following information:

— the name of the limited partnership;

— the address of its office and the name and address of its agent for service of process;

— the name and address of each general partner;

— the latest date on which the limited partnership may dissolve; and

— any other matters the general partners decide to include.

Under RULPA (1985), the name of the limited partnership must include the words "Limited Partnership," but in many states, the abbreviation "L.P." will suffice to put third parties on notice that the liability of the owners is limited.

A limited partnership is formed when the Certificate is filed by the Secretary of State if there has been substantial compliance with the statutory requirements. If no Certificate has been filed by the Secretary of State before business commences, the business is a *general partnership*, the default form for a business with more than one owner.

If no Certificate has been filed by the Secretary of State, someone who mistakenly believes he is a limited partner can avoid *future* liability by submitting a Certificate himself or by withdrawing from the limited partnership and notifying the Secretary of State of his withdrawal, but he cannot escape liability that has *already* arisen (*i.e.*, neither the newly-filed Certificate nor the withdrawal has retroactive effect).

D. Limited Partnership Agreement

As indicated above, RULPA (1985) anticipates that there will be a written partnership agreement that addresses contributions, finances, the relationship among the partners, and other important matters about the partnership's internal affairs. Some states require a written partnership agreement, although RULPA does not.

A partnership agreement is not a public document, so a diligent third party will want to request a copy before making a loan or extending credit to the firm. That is good advice for anyone who is dealing with a limited partnership: CYA ("Cover you're a--") in advance!

E. Capital Contributions

A partner may make a capital contribution in virtually any form—cash, property, services rendered, a promissory note, or an obligation to contribute cash or property or to perform services. (Usually, limited partners contribute capital and general partners provide skills and know-how, but general partners may contribute capital, too.) However, a limited partner's promise to contribute is enforceable only if it is set out in a *signed writing*.

F.   Profits and Losses/Voting Rights

Profits and losses are allocated according to the written partnership agreement. If the written partnership agreement does not provide for an allocation, profits and losses are shared pro rata based on the value of the partners' capital contributions. This rule is different from the default rules for general partnerships, where partners split profits equally unless otherwise agreed, and losses follow profits. Voting rights are left to the partnership agreement; the statute does not provide a default rule.

G.   Admission of New Partners

After the Certificate has been filed, additional general partners may be admitted as provided in the written partnership agreement or, if the agreement does not provide for the admission of additional general partners, on the written consent of *all* the partners. Likewise, additional limited partners may be admitted on compliance with the partnership agreement, or if the partnership agreement does not so provide, on the written consent of *all* the partners.

H.   Withdrawal of a Partner

In the Lone Star state, it is often said, "Once a Texan, always a Texan." That may be true for a Longhorn, but it is not necessarily the case for partners in a limited partnership. A general partner can withdraw from the limited partnership at any time by giving written notice to the other partners. However, if the withdrawal is in breach of the limited partnership agreement (a "wrongful" withdrawal), the withdrawing general partner is liable for damages, just as he would be in a general partnership.

A limited partner may withdraw from the limited partnership at any time specified or on the occurrence of an event specified in writing in the limited partnership agreement. However, if the agreement is silent on withdrawal, a limited partner may withdraw by giving not less than six months' written notice to *each* general partner. It is easy to become a limited partner, but not so easy to get out!

I. Role of Limited Partnerships Today

Today, limited partnerships are used mainly for one of two purposes: (1) to shield assets from federal estate tax in a Family Limited Partnership or (2) as a vehicle to raise venture capital.

In a Family Limited Partnership, parents form a limited partnership with themselves as the general partners, contribute real estate to the limited partnership, and gift their children limited partnership interests. Because limited partners cannot exercise control, the children's interests are valued at only a fraction of the property's worth. When the parents die, the market value of the property is not included in their estate; only the much lower value of the limited partnership interests is included. This perfectly legitimate arrangement can save wealthy families a lot of money at the expense of the IRS.

Venture capital firms invest money in start-up technology companies, hoping to make a killing when the start-up goes public at some point in the future. Venture capital firms are traditionally formed as limited partnerships.

J.   Limited Liability Limited Partnerships

One of the main liabilities (pun intended) of operating a business as a limited partnership is that the general partners are personally liable for the firm's obligations. However, these days there is a way to avoid that albatross: form a **limited liability limited partnership (LLLP)**. A limited liability partnership is exactly like a limited partnership except in one major respect: the *general partners* are shielded from vicarious liability. The extent of the general partners' liability depends on whether the state of formation has a narrow shield (limits only vicarious tort liability) or a broad shield statute (limits vicarious liability for both torts and contracts). Think of an LLLP as a limited partnership without personal liability for the general partners (**LLLP = LP – personal liability for general partners**).

A limited liability limited partnership is a hybrid business form: it combines a limited partnership (which shields limited partners) with a limited liability partnership (which shields general partners). It's like 1 + 2 = 3: **LP + LLP = LLLP** (note the corresponding number of "L"s in each of those partnership names). Insulating general partners from personal liability is another reflection of the modern trend discussed above in connection with limited liability partnerships: protecting the owners of a business from personal liability at the expense of those who do business with the firm.

K.   Concluding Thoughts on Limited Partnerships

Some final thoughts before leaving limited partnerships. Although most publicly traded businesses are organized as corporations, some limited partnerships, known as Master Limited Partnerships, are public companies. Master Limited Partnerships are taxed like corporations under the Internal Revenue Code (subject to exceptions set out in the Code). They do not get the benefit of pass-through taxation afforded to most partnerships.

Also, for the record, limited partnership interests are considered "securities" for the purpose of federal securities law. As a result, the registration and anti-fraud provisions of federal securities law may apply, resulting in rescission, damages, and in some cases, even criminal liability for persons selling interests in a limited partnership.

Finally, keep in mind that if you are going to use the limited partnership as your business form of choice, make sure it is a *limited liability limited partnership*. Why put the general partners' assets at risk, when it is so easy to shield them from the grasp of the firm's creditors?

PART IV

Choice of Business Form: LLP or LLC?

Deciding which kind of business association to utilize today usually boils down to the choice between a limited liability partnership ("LLP") and a limited liability company ("LLC"). The three primary concerns for people going into business together tend to implicate the following issues:

(1) limiting their personal liability (and the personal liability of any investors) for the firm's obligations;

(2) minimizing their federal income tax liability; and

(3) maintaining control of the business.

Other types of business association are deficient in one or more of these respects.

— A general partnership is undesirable because partners in a general partnership are subject to *personal liability* for the firm's obligations.

— A limited partnership is unsatisfactory in most states because general partners are *personally liable* for firm obligations and the limited partners *cannot*

> *participate in control* without risking personal liability.

— A corporation is problematic because the corporation and its shareholders may end up paying *more federal income tax* collectively than if the business were operated in unincorporated form. Corporate income is potentially taxed *twice*, once at the entity level and again at the shareholder level if that income is distributed to shareholders in the form of a dividend ("double taxation").

For these reasons, neither a general partnership, a limited partnership or a corporation is likely to be the business form of choice today.

By contrast, we saw earlier that an LLP allows its owners to accomplish all three objectives, namely, limited personal liability, pass-through tax treatment, and a flexible management structure (the partners can agree on how the LLP will be run.) An LLC offers the same advantages: limited liability for the owners ("members"), pass-through tax treatment and flexible management structure. Accordingly, it is appropriate to consider why a business owner would prefer an LLP to an LLC or vice versa.

A. Historical Comparison

Initially, circumstances favored the LLP. Texas enacted the first LLP statute in the country in 1991. Many general partnerships rushed to register as LLPs to take advantage of the LLP's liability shield. Under the Internal Revenue Code, LLPs, like other partnerships, get *conduit* tax treatment. An LLP does not pay federal income tax on its income. The LLP's income is instead *passed through* to the partners, who pay tax on it at their own individual federal income tax rates.

By contrast, prior to 1997, the Internal Revenue Service assessed on a case-by-case basis whether an LLC would be taxed like a partnership or like a corporation. The resulting uncertainty provided a disincentive to operate a business as an LLC. However, in 1997, the IRS conceded. It announced that an LLC could ensure conduit taxation by simply checking a box on an IRS form (referred to as the IRS's "check-the-box" regulation).

Today, LLCs need not even check a box. They are granted conduit taxation *by default.*

Once the IRS threw in the towel, there was finally a level playing field for LLPs and LLCs when it came to federal income taxation. Nonetheless, lack of familiarity with the LLC statute and the absence of caselaw precedent weighed against using an LLC. Obviously, those disadvantages of the LLC have disappeared over time.

B. Benefits of Using an LLC

Once the LLC got the imprimatur of the IRS, the LLC became wildly popular. In fact, the LLC is the preferred form of business association in the United States today. There are several reasons why the LLC eclipsed the LLP as the business form of choice:

(1) In a state with a narrow shield LLP statute, it makes sense to opt for an LLC, which shields partners from vicarious liability for contracts as well as vicarious liability for torts. Why get a partial shield when you can a full one?

(2) In some states, like New York and California, only persons who provide professional services (like lawyers and accountants) may form an LLP, so the LLC became the vehicle of choice for non-professionals in those jurisdictions.

(3) In many states, the LLC statute allows greater flexibility to contract around default rules, including the rules pertaining to the fiduciary duties of members and managers. *Freedom of contract* is the quintessential hallmark of an LLC.

(4) There are many fewer governance rules for LLCs than there are for corporations. If the owners of a business want to maximize flexibility, the LLC is likely to be the better option for their business.

(5) If a firm has only one owner, it cannot operate as an LLP since a partnership, by definition, must have two or more persons as co-owners.

C. (Minor) Downsides of Using an LLC

Unlike the UPA and RUPA, the Uniform Limited Liability Company Act ("ULLCA") was not widely adopted, in part because most states had enacted LLC statutes before the ULLCA was promulgated. As a result, there is far more variation among state LLC statutes than among state partnership statutes.

Some states also require the LLC to pay more in fees than the LLP, but in the long run, these fees are relatively insignificant. They are not much of a disincentive to operate as an LLC.

Another issue concerns the way LLCs are managed. Some states adopted a *corporate model* in their LLC statutes. Under that model, *managers* manage the LLC's business unless otherwise provided in the Registration Statement on file with the Secretary of State or in an operating agreement among the members. This centralized management structure resembles a corporation's board of directors. Other states adopted a *partnership model* where the members run the LLC unless otherwise provided in the Registration Statement or operating agreement. This decentralized management structure resembles a partnership. Some states allow management to be divided between members and managers. In any event, regardless of what the default rule is in a given state, the owners may always contract around it.

A lingering question with respect to LLCs concerns how a court should handle issues on which the statute is silent. If a legal issue arises that is not addressed in the LLC statute, should the court treat the issue the way it would treat a *partnership* or the way it would treat a *corporation*? There is no hard and fast rule. Many courts will look at the structure of the LLC to answer this inquiry. If the LLC is managed by managers, those courts will tend to apply corporate principles to resolve the issue. In contrast, if the LLC is managed by members, those courts will tend to adopt partnership rules to resolve the issue.

Other courts take a more *ad hoc* approach that varies with the specific issue involved in the case. For example, if an creditor of an LLC seeks to hold the members personally liable on an LLC obligation, the court may look to the corporate law doctrine of piercing the corporate veil as the closest analogue.

Given the disparate approaches taken by courts, there is still some uncertainty in this area. Over time, however, these issues are likely to be resolved, leaving one less impediment to operating in the form of an LLC.

PART V

A Final Note

It is important to recognize that regardless of what kind of business form you choose, you can always *merge* or *convert* it into a *different* business form if the circumstances warrant. Hopefully, with the knowledge you have gained in this book, you will be more attuned to which type of business association is most advantageous for you or your client. Good luck on your exam and in all your professional endeavors!